CHOICE POINT

**BREAK THE CYCLE OF SELF-SABOTAGE,
ACCELERATE YOUR GROWTH, AND REALIZE
YOUR TRUE POTENTIAL**

RYAN SAWYER

My sincerest gratitude to my wife, Heidi, for her love and support throughout my ongoing transformation and the sharing of this story. Thank you to my writing coach, Laurel, who cheered me on and helped me navigate the writing process.

CONTENTS

INTRODUCTION

Are you in transition or contemplating a big life change? Are you struggling with irritability, tired of riding a roller coaster of emotions, or just sick of beating yourself up?

If you're like I was, you may be thinking that there must be more to life than feeling stuck and torn between work and your home life.

Maybe you're recognizing that the way you've been living isn't working for you anymore. Even though you want a different experience of life, you feel like a hypocrite, continually sabotaging your happiness.

I wrote this book to serve as an example of how it's possible to let go of the stories that are no longer serving you and to instead become the author of your own life.

I've realized that if there is just one tiny crack of light shining onto the deep dark aspect of ourselves, it will cast a shadow that we can look at, objectify, and decide whether it is our truth.

My hope is for you to fall in love with the process of growth and fully embrace all there is to experience in each moment. If I were to sum up all of this in one word, it would be freedom. Freedom to rewrite the narrative of your story, freedom from unnecessary suffering, freedom to create space for limitless possibilities and a life that's greater than you could have ever imagined.

MY STORY OF TRANSFORMATION

*When you've experienced depression and anxiety
throughout your whole life, you don't think anything
is ever going to change. It feels like that is who you are,
and you just learn to suppress it and to hide it. When
I left college coaching, it wasn't to stop experiencing
depression. It was so that I could start the biggest fight
of my life. It was to save my life.*

I was living my dream, being a defensive line college football coach. Coaching football was the only thing I'd ever wanted to do with my life. I remember in my teenage years dreaming of someday being national champion. I never expected I would do anything else. I loved every minute of it; it was me, my identity, what I was born to do! I had a vision of making it to the highest level, and nothing was going to stop me.

The height of my coaching career was the 2010 national championship season. It was a magical season, to say the least—like something out of a movie. We were the most resilient team I had ever witnessed, and we had a mentality that was second to none. If there was any chance we could win, we would find a way. Speaking of finding a way: As a defensive line, we drew the short straw for meeting rooms that year, and because our facilities were under construction, we had to get creative. We turned an old storage room into a meeting room that we called "the dungeon." It was dimly lit and cold, with old wooden chairs, fold-up tables, a portable projector screen, and extension cords running everywhere. We grew to take pride in "the dungeon." It represented the grit of that year's team perfectly.

I remember vividly a conversation I had with our head coach as we walked out of our first winter workout in preparation for the 2010 season. I turned to him and said, "There is something different about this team, did you feel that?"

He replied "Yes, there is something special about this team!" There's no way I could cover all of the details about that season here; it would take an entire book to tell you about each pivotal moment when it seemed we were doomed—and someone would make a game-saving play. It was one incredible comeback win after another.

So, when we found ourselves down 19–0 in the national champion-ship game, without our best offensive player, it was the perfect setup for one more comeback to finish our storybook season. I remember wondering how we were going to pull this one out, up until the middle of the third quarter. We were getting our ass kicked in every aspect of the game.

I'll never forget the moment I realized we would find a way one more time. We'd just made a three-and-out stop on defense. I was watching one of the opposing team's offensive linemen getting off the ground slowly, suffering from cramps. I ran down to my brother TJ, who was watching on the sidelines, grabbed him by the arm, and said, "We got their ass." He looked at me as if I were crazy. Maybe I was, but I knew our team, and if you gave us just a tiny bit of hope, we would find a way—it was just a matter of how! And that's exactly what happened. We made three unanswered scores, and it was now the final drive of the fourth quarter. We had to make one more defensive stop, as we had so many times that season. Our defense got them into a fourth and ten. They took a timeout. Thinking of it now, I can still feel the nerves and excitement of the conversation I had with the defensive coordinator: Do we rush four or bring pressure? The defensive coor-dinator said, "Let's finish this thing." We decided on the play call: "G follow Peel." It was a pressure that we had added to our scheme just a few weeks before. If they ran the protection we were expecting, they wouldn't be able to block us. The play started, and we got it right, forc-ing a bad throw and stopping them two yards short of a first down. I remember feeling like I didn't want to let my guard down. Was it real? Did we do it?

We were national champions. My childhood dream had come true. As everybody rushed onto the field, the excitement overcame me, and I dropped to my knees with a sense of relief and amazement for what we'd accomplished. This was quickly followed by a voice in my head saying, "We've got to do that again!" This experience added to the feeling of confidence that I was doing the right thing with my life. I thought, I belong here. It was the pinnacle of my coaching career.

Just the other day, my son Colton, age seven, was bored on a rainy afternoon and started digging through an old box underneath his bed. He found some memorabilia from my playing and coaching days. He came to me with some photos and a DVD in his hand. He started asking questions.

"Dad, is that you?"

"Yes."

"What is this DVD?"

"That's a movie from when your Dad was part of a very special team."

"Can we watch it?" he asked excitedly.

As we sat down to watch the documentary of the 2010 season, I was slightly nervous, not sure how I was going to feel revisiting that time in my life. Colton was excited to see his dad on TV, although when I flashed across the screen, he didn't recognize me—storming around, intense look on my face, 70 pounds heavier. I barely recognized myself. As we watched, I felt a wide range of emotions, from feeling incredibly proud of that season and my coaching career to empathy for that version of myself that was hiding so much guilt and anger. I found myself wondering, Did he know how much he was suppressing? I saw myself from an entirely different perspective. I was looking at a man who had no idea of the journey he was about to undertake. I wished I could offer him guidance or give him the awareness and tools he would need. It was like looking back at a different life.

When we finished watching the documentary, Colton asked, "Dad, why don't you still coach?"

"My life took an unexpected turn, buddy. I was meant for something else."

MOTIVATION

Motivation starts with a whisper

In March 2011, following the national championship, Heidi and I got married at a lakeside resort in Priest Lake, Idaho. It was a fantastic weekend of celebration with friends and family. The championship trophy was even there on the mantle during the whole weekend so we could take pictures holding it.

We didn't wait long to start a family. Colton was born in the middle of the 2012 season. Talk about a crazy time: I brought Heidi and baby Colton home from the hospital on a Friday, then jumped in a car and drove to Bozeman to coach in a game against Montana State on Saturday. Both teams were ranked in the top 10 nationally at the time. Just in case you were wondering, we handled business in Bozeman. Seventeen months later, we were blessed by the arrival of our second child, a baby girl, Hailey Mae.

From 2012 until I finally decided to walk away from coaching in 2015 my inner turmoil went from manageable to a state of desperation as I tried to figure out how to continue to hide the pain I was in. I had massive anxiety attacks and spells of depression that lasted longer and longer. Having a wife and two beautiful babies at home brought everything to the surface. I wanted to be healthy and enjoy my life with them. Many times the depression was so bad that I struggled to even get on the floor and play with my kids. I wanted so badly to be home and more involved as a father. I no longer wanted to live the lifestyle of a college football coach.

I could especially see the impact that my career was having on my son. From the time Colton was a baby, every time I left the room, he would scream and cry. This separation anxiety persisted, and I began noticing a sense of sadness in him when he was only two years old. He just kind of moped around at times, and this mood seemed to come on without warning. One moment he would be playing with his toys or engaging with someone in the room, and the next he would isolate himself and look lost. I remember one time he was playing with blocks in the living room. He was content, as only a two-year-old can be, and suddenly there was a complete shift in his body language—his shoulders slumped, his head dropped. He looked at the wooden block in his hand, his expression went blank, and then he dropped the block.

Heidi and I looked at each other, and she asked, "Is he okay?"

I turned and watched him closely. It was like déjà vu. It was as if I were watching myself at his age. I could see it in his eyes, and it scared me. I thought, I have to figure this out. I need to learn how to deal with this in a healthy manner, so when he reaches the age when I began battling, I can be there for him. I need to be able to support him, to answer the questions he's going to have.

HIDING IN THE DARKNESS

*It's dark and lonely. My eyes feel heavy, my shoulders
are hunched, and I feel like I'm on the verge of tears.
I'm not worthy of anything. The world is better off
without me. If I wake up tomorrow feeling like this,
I'm ending it.*

One day, as I was doing the dishes, it hit me like a ton of bricks. A tightness in my throat grew until I could barely breathe. I felt a heaviness in my chest, and I couldn't see. It felt as if the world were collapsing and closing in around me. I thought, What is happening to me? I had dealt with anxiety my whole life, but this was different, this was downright scary. I stumbled away from the sink and sat on the floor in the corner of the next room, curled up in a ball, trying to hide and let it pass.

That's when Heidi found me. She came into the room and asked, "What's going on, why are you curled up like that?" She had no idea that I had been battling anxiety and depression for most of my life. Now I had to tell her; I couldn't hide anymore.

"I've had these anxiety attacks recently, and they are getting worse. I was trying to hide so you and the kids wouldn't see it."

She sat down, got quiet, and just watched me.

I continued, "I've been dealing with this for years, but it's gotten much worse in the past few months. I'm in a lot of pain. I've even thought of ending it all."

She looked dazed and overwhelmed.

"Why didn't you tell me about this?"

"I was ashamed and embarrassed." The tension grew.

"How did I not notice? How long has this been going on?"

I felt utterly guilty and ashamed: guilty about exposing Heidi and the kids to this and ashamed that I'd hidden it from her in the first place. I felt like a fraud.

"I'm not the man you think you married," I said. I proceeded to tell her the whole story, starting with my first memories of depression and anxiety as a teenager.

I was a sophomore in high school, 16 years old, a football player trying to live up to all kinds of expectations. During fall camp, I'd gone six days without eating because I was so anxious. I had tried but couldn't get a single bite of food down. At practice, I was standing in a drill line when blood started running out of my nose. My position coach looked at me and asked, "Are you ok?" At that moment, my knees went weak and I collapsed. I had exhausted myself completely. I'd lost 17 pounds in six days. I had no idea that this was a warning sign.

One day, when I was 18, I found the longest stretch in the parking lot at my high school. I unbuckled the seat belt in my Nissan pickup and floored it, across the parking lot. Just before I hit the pole I was aiming for, a voice in my head screamed, No! I hit the brakes and swerved out of danger.

In college, I spent a lot of time partying and drinking. At the end of the night, I'd finish off whatever booze was within reach, hoping I wouldn't wake up the next morning. I most often experienced suicidal thoughts when I was on the freeway—I would get the urge to turn into oncoming traffic.

At 22, I sought help. I told a doctor about these extreme lows and explained how I could barely stand being in my own skin. The doctor asked a few questions, prescribed some medication, and sent me on my way. I took the medication for a couple of years, but eventually I just got tired of walking around feeling like a zombie.

In the years that followed, I secretly sought out therapy multiple times. I would tell the therapist what I was experiencing. Although it seemed to help in the moment, nothing really changed. So, I just began to accept it. This is who I am, this is my deal, I'll ride high and then I'll crash.

I'd been on this roller coaster ever since, and had gotten somewhat accustomed to its ups and downs. But lately, the downs had lasted longer and longer.

As I shared all of this with Heidi, I felt a sense of relief: I didn't have to hide it anymore. There was also a slight movement of energy in my chest around my heart, as if I had removed a rock from a stream. I'd released my grip on a certain part of myself that I'd been holding onto, and it was finally able to flow.

This was the beginning of a long and bumpy road for Heidi and me. But eventually it would lead us back to each other, stronger than before.

GROWING GUILT

Guilt, this is what I felt with every breath. I felt guilty for being alive. I felt guilty for feeling guilty. I even woke up feeling guilty. Every conversation made me feel guilty, and I wasn't sure why, but this was my existence.

Deep down, I knew I couldn't beat the depression and continue to coach. However, I was in a lot of anguish over the decision to quit. The thought of moving on without football was terrifying; it was my life. Being a college football coach is a very demanding job, it's all in or nothing. So if I was going to fight this, I would have to stop coaching and focus on getting healthy. I couldn't continue to be the coach I wanted to be and save my own life, too.

I was afraid. What would people think? Would people assume that I had gotten fired? What would become of my reputation? I didn't want to disappoint my colleagues, players, family, and friends. I was living my dream job and working for an incredible head coach, who had become one of my best friends. He was the reason I even had the chance to be a coach. He had hired me when no one else would. Long ago, he had assured me that if he ever became a head coach, I would be his first hire—and he kept his word. I felt like I owed him to continue to show up and produce.

I felt guilty for letting the players down. I didn't want them to see me as a quitter, or weak. I was also worried about the effect on all my relationships: with my father, my brothers, my extended family, my friends. It was this cool thing for them, watching me live out my dream on the field on game days. Football had brought many people into my life. It had also brought my friends and family together. So many people were proud of me for being a coach. To strip myself of all that by choice was gut wrenching.

Heidi and I went back and forth leading up to my decision, and I nearly drove her nuts during our late-night conversations. "I think I need to walk away, but what if I do, what will that look like? Worst of all, what if I leave my childhood dream job and can't find happiness?" And on and on. Heidi was always supportive but was careful to take a neutral stance. She wanted to make sure she wasn't persuading me to go one way or another.

WALKING AWAY

When we tell the truth of ourselves, there is no more hiding, no more clinging to false identities. When we tell the truth of ourselves, we let go and surrender to the unknown.

On the Monday following the 2015 season, our worst season to date, our head coach called a meeting. He had given us coaches an assignment. We were to assess ourselves and our positions for the year. How were we going to be more structured? What was our plan to develop our position? And over the winter, what would we implement? What kind of things would we do, and how would we schedule them? How would we stay on top of the players' academics? It was a full assessment of every aspect of what we were doing as coaches. I sat down to write on that Monday morning and froze. I couldn't get two words on the screen.

I thought, I just can't do it. I knew that if I wrote it, I'd be lying to him. After a couple of hours of sitting there, battling with myself, I got a call from Connor, one of my closest friends. I had told him I was going to give my notice that day.

He asked, "Did you do it?"

"Not yet," I said.

"What are you waiting for? You know what you have to do. You know this is the right thing for you."

Right after that call, I walked into my head coach's office.

"Hey, boss, we need to talk," I said. I closed the door and took a seat on the couch.

He looked at me. "Everything alright?"

"No. I just don't have it anymore."

"Ok, What does that mean?" He asked

"Do you remember our conversation a year ago when I told you there was something off with me and I wasn't sure how to handle it? You recognized that I am really hard on myself and encouraged me to find ways to have more grace and patience with myself."

"Yes, of course."

"The Guilt and anxiety that I was feeling then has only Intensified. I need to figure this out."

"How about you take some personal time?" Then we can talk more after recruiting season."

"No, you don't understand. I'm in such a bad spot mentally and emotionally that I don't want to be here anymore. I'm barely holding it together," I said.

"Okay," he said. "You've gotta do what's right for you. Let me know if there is anything I can do."

"You've done everything you can," I said. "Thank you for being so understanding, and thank you for all the opportunities and the memories. Now my life is about fighting this."

I went around to each coach's office to tell them my story, to explain what I had been battling. I called an emergency meeting with my position players to let them know I was walking away and to tell them that I couldn't take care of myself and my family and be the coach they needed me to be. I assured them that they had gotten everything they needed from me and that the next coach would make them even better. It was a very emotional meeting. When it was over, I went into my office, cleared out my desk, and left. I felt entirely sure I was doing the right thing, but at the same time I felt like I was losing my identity.

As I opened the door to leave for good, I felt myself take a breath: it seemed like the first breath of my life. I chose myself over what others thought of me; I put my life and my family first. I got into my car. Looking back at the office building one last time, I felt a powerful sense of loss. As I drove the 15 minutes to my home, I felt myself physically hit a wall and barely made it inside the house. I went straight to bed and slept for nearly the entire week.

PHYSICAL TRANSFORMATION

***No matter how hard we push ourselves physically,
real transformation isn't possible until we take an
integrated approach.***

Leaving coaching was not the final turning point, not at all. The week after I left coaching was Thanksgiving, and a lot was going on at home. The kids were one and three years old, and life was busy! Heidi had been introduced to some nutritional products that were working well for both of us. She believed we could create another income stream through sharing them with others. The business model was network marketing. She'd been working hard over the past several months to earn income during my transition. I joined in, working full time with Heidi for six months on building out our business. Around the time I left coaching, we hit the highest leadership rank in the company, which meant we were eligible for bonuses, and there was potential for making some legitimate money. I was at a place in my transformation where I was speaking about my depression to anybody and everybody that would listen. I was no longer hiding it.

So, I got on the phone and started telling old friends and connections what was going on. I told them about my struggles with depression, and then I'd tell them about the nutritional system that was helping me get healthy.

By the time we first started using these nutritional products about a year before I left coaching, I had already tried multiple things to help relieve my anxiety; for example, I'd cut out gluten and quit drinking alcohol. These adjustments seemed to provide my body with just a little bit of room to breathe—a little bit of hope. So, I shifted my focus and dialed in on nutrition and physical fitness.

I lost a total of 70 pounds. Even though I was in the best shape of my life physically, the depression continued to worsen. In the beginning, I thought there was something inside of me that had to be beaten out of me. Every three or four days I'd do one of what I called my "exorcisms." I'd push myself to complete exhaustion to get it out of me. I would look in the mirror, screaming, Get the fuck out of me, I don't want you in me anymore! I would have a physical release that reminded me of the movie The Green Mile when the man opened his mouth and it looked like flies came out. That's what it felt like, this external release coming out through my mouth. I would experience some peace for a few days and then the darkness would return. At the time, those were the only tools I had—strict nutrition and extreme physical exercise. I thought that was the answer. I thought that was transformation. I just needed to continue to push myself harder and harder. On the outside, I looked super healthy and fit, but I was still dying on the inside.

SELF-SABOTAGE

If we don't wake up to our conditioning, we will
unconsciously sabotage everything good in our life.

Eventually, the business Heidi and I were working in together stalled out because we just weren't vibing together. The transition to me being home had proven to be bumpier than I had anticipated. We weren't used to spending so much time together; I'd been a coach our entire relationship and that meant I wasn't home much. Heidi didn't understand my struggle and didn't know how to support me in my fight with depression. I became certified as a Spartan SGX coach, thinking it would be the perfect combination of coaching others through their physical fitness transformation and providing them with nutritional support. I was obsessed with my reinvention. Heidi and I began to grow apart. Her uncertainty about how to handle our situation led me to believe she didn't love me anymore.

During this time, I met a woman through Spartan coaching. We started training and coaching together and became very close friends. She listened and validated my struggles. She seemed to know what to say to help me feel safe. I found myself drawing closer to her for support, and eventually it grew into an emotionally entangled relationship. Thank God, Heidi is a strong-willed woman. Heidi knew something was going on and confronted me. I completely expected her to leave me; I didn't expect her to fight since I had convinced myself she didn't love me. Her reaction showed me a side of her that I was blind to, a strength I didn't see before.

I had almost manifested my biggest fear, losing my wife and my family. I'd always had this underlying belief that I didn't deserve to be happy and that I wasn't good enough to have someone who would love me unconditionally. I was afraid of having everything I ever wanted because deep down I was always waiting for the other shoe to drop. I assumed that eventually history would repeat itself, and I would fuck it up. The depression had such a grip on me. I believed that no matter what I did, sooner or later, I would lose the fight; sooner or later, the depression would win.

I was sabotaging myself; I was sabotaging my marriage; I was destroying my life. No matter what I changed about my life or my physical appearance, I was getting in return exactly how I treated myself. My unconscious beliefs and patterns were being exposed.

While this was going on, I noticed my throat would sometimes close up, and I would have episodes of choking on food. I had a suspicion that I was really sick, and I was secretly rooting for it. It got to the point where I couldn't even swallow a protein shake; I was continually choking due to my esophagus swelling shut. I remember thinking, You have throat cancer. All those years of chewing tobacco and drinking have finally caught up with you— nice job, asshole! I postponed going to the doctor because deep down I didn't want them to catch it. I believed this was my way out. I wouldn't have to fight anymore, I wouldn't have to face my failing marriage and what I had put Heidi through. I could just be a victim and have an excuse for my departure.

After I choked and needed the Heimlich maneuver at a friend's wedding, Heidi convinced me to go to the doctor. We had some tests done; it wasn't cancer. I needed a procedure to expand my esophagus, and afterward they gave me some dietary restrictions. Heidi was by my side every step of the way, even though it was clear that our future as a couple was very uncertain. While I was in the hospital bed, waiting for the procedure, I looked at her and thought, What are you still doing here? I was so unable to love myself, how could she?

WHY DID THAT WORK?

You are going to take this pain, and you are going to transmute it! You are going to transform! There has got to be some sort of positive thing that can come out of all of this.

Heidi's loyalty and strength gave me the hope I needed to start to wake up. I made a vow to Heidi and myself. I'm going as far as I have to go. I'm going to try anything. I'm going to find a way to beat this!

Soon after this awakening, I started a residential painting company, so we had some financial stability. In the process, I decided to join a business networking group. The group had weekly meetings with all of the members, and then we'd break off and do one-on-one meetings with individual members to build relationships.

I had a meeting with a woman from the group, and we ended up going into our stories. I told her about leaving coaching and my depression.

"Oh, depression, that's easy," she said.

I looked at her like, you've got to be kidding me.

She continued, "All you have to do is ask yourself a simple question. Why am I so happy? Ask yourself out loud three times, like you mean it, with a smile on your face, and you won't be depressed anymore."

How dare you tell me this is easy! I thought. I wrapped up the meeting quickly, completely disgusted that someone would tell me what I was going through was easy.

As I drove away, furious, I talked to myself: "Well, Ryan, you told yourself that you are willing to try anything—what do you have to lose? So, go ahead and say it!"

I mumbled with resistance, "Why am I so happy, why am I so happy, why am I so happy?"

I thought, That's not it, she said to speak it out loud, and smile. So, I tried again. This time loudly, "Why am I so happy? Why am I so happy? Why am I so happy?"

I wasn't smiling and I didn't say it with much enthusiasm, but I noticed this slight twinge. And I was like, what was that? It was like something moved. Energy moved. I thought to myself, Well, do it one time all out just like you committed to yourself you'd do. Just completely commit and believe it's true.

So, I smiled, and loudly, almost yelling, said, "Why am I so happy? Why am I so happy? Why am I so happy?" And I felt this vibration in my body. I felt this lift, and I started laughing. It worked! Only for a moment, but it did work.

Why did it work?

I need to know why.

THE COLLECTIVE MENTORS

"You cannot transit wisdom and insight to another person. The seed is already there. A good teacher touches the seed, allowing it to wake up, to sprout, and to grow."

- Thich Nhat Hanh

I became very curious about how the human brain works and wanted to study and learn so that I could make sense of my experience. I was suddenly fascinated with being a student of life and making myself an experiment. And I had questions, lots of questions. When I started to ask them, the answers came through a multitude of sources: mentors, coaches, authors, podcasts, signs, and synchronicities.

Combined, they became what I call the voice of my Collective Mentors (CM). When I looked back over my journals at the things I'd learned about the freedom I found, it was like I was in a conversation with this collective mentor. I'd have a question, and the answer would come as if it were always there. Every answer seemed to be exactly what I needed to hear when I needed to hear it.

The following is a glimpse into that conversation that took place over the years as I searched for the answers to my questions.

Me: What's this voice in my head? Where did it come from?

CM: Michael Singer writes about it in his book The Untethered Soul. He calls it the "roommate" that won't shut up. I think that's accurate. The truth is, it is a part of you, but it is not who you are.

Me: Who am I, then?

CM: You are the one who hears the voice in your head. You are the witness.

Me: I'm not sure I understand.

CM: To understand this entirely, you will need to develop a practice of witnessing your thoughts. Just observe your thoughts without attaching to them or trying to stop them. Just let them come and go and bring yourself back to the present moment. In time, you will sense yourself as the witness and not that voice. This is where your work begins.

I did as I was instructed and developed a practice of witnessing my thoughts. It gave me insight into recognizing one of the primary conversations that were continuously running in my head. I noticed the stories that pointed toward feeling guilty. The thoughts in my head kept repeating: You're not a good father. You need to be a better husband. You don't deserve this, and sooner or later you will fuck it up.

Me: Why am I always feeling guilty about everything?

CM: Those thoughts and feelings were programmed into you from a very early age. You took on limiting beliefs about yourself in childhood. That guilt is just an experience you are having. It is not who you are.

David Hawkins pinpoints it in his book Letting Go: "Feelings of guilt are always associated with a feeling of wrongness and potential punishment, either real or in fantasy. If punishment is not forthcoming in the external world it expresses itself as self-punishment on an emotional level. It is a learned behavior which is purportedly pragmatic: to prevent further error or the repetition of a mistake. Ninety-nine percent of guilt has nothing whatsoever to do with reality."

I thought about this for a while. It was freeing to understand that this guilt was something I was experiencing, but it wasn't me. It was an illusion—just a loop running in my head. I began to be able to witness what was happening and bring myself into the present moment without judgment.

Me: I still don't understand why the programs ran and why it is so hard to change them?

CM: As I said earlier, these programs took root early on in your life and were reinforced for decades. They are literally programmed into the very cells of your being.

Me: That doesn't sound good.

CM: It's not as bad as it seems, but it does explain why it's so difficult to change. Dr. Joe Dispenza explains it in detail in his book Breaking the Habit of Being Yourself, but I'll summarize it for you. It is estimated that people think some 60,000–70,000 thoughts a day. And of those thoughts, over 80 percent are the same thoughts as yesterday. When we think a thought, a series of things happen in the brain. Neurons are fired, chemicals are released, genes are signaled, connections are made, networks are established, cells are programmed to respond in specific ways to match the way you are feeling and thinking. For example, if you are thinking positive thoughts such as joy or love, you turn on a certain set of circuits in your brain (the ones that ran the last time you thought these thoughts). If you do this for a long time, you create deep neurological pathways or programs. Over time, these programs begin to run on their own, triggered by your external or internal environment.

Me. That still seems a little vague...

CM: Remember when you coached football how you used drills to instill habits in your players? And in the big moment of the championship game, they did exactly what you trained them to do—just by relying on instinct? That happened because the brain and body had been programmed. Conscious thinking wasn't required. In fact, you probably wouldn't have won that championship if conscious thinking was required. It takes too long.

Me: Okay, I think I get it.

CM: Now, another critical thing to understand: It is not just the thought but the associated feeling that is crucial. If you think of the thought as an electrical impulse and the feeling as a magnet, it will help you understand. In the brain, your thought fires the neuron, and the chemicals released create the feeling.

Now consider the consequences if the program is a negative one. For example, the program that runs when you have thoughts that trigger feelings of guilt. You have the thought (neurons are fired and wired together), chemicals (hormones) are released, you begin to feel the way you are thinking, so you attract another negative thought (remember, the feeling is like a magnet and the stronger the feeling, the stronger the draw). Neurons are again fired and wired, chemicals are released, and now your feeling matches the way you are thinking. This loop continues: thought, feeling, feeling, thought, and so on, until you have a very efficient network of cellular connections that run on their own without the conscious mind ever knowing.

And now, we are back to why you must witness your thoughts; the only way to stop this cycle is to interrupt the thoughts. In football terms, you must intercept the pass before it is completed.

So, I worked on witnessing my thoughts and intercepting the negative ones. I was getting pretty good at it, but as soon as I started feeling good, I met with tremendous resistance.

Me: Why am I meeting with such resistance when I try to change my thinking?

CM: Remember what I said about the chemicals that are released in your body when you think and feel a certain way?

Me: Yeah.

CM: Well, the longer you think and the stronger you feel about what you are thinking, the more chemicals are released, and the deeper and more solid the neurological pathways become. For instance, that guilty thought/feeling mix you have been running in your mind for decades. That's a pretty strong habit mixture by now, don't you think?

Me: Yeah, it is!

CM: Well, you may not want to hear this, but you are addicted to that mixture of guilty thoughts and guilty feelings. Your body and mind have been running that program so long that the body has a memory of it at the cellular level. When you try to change that program, it will resist—strongly!

Me: So that's why it's so hard to stop. It makes sense. But I don't like the idea that I'm addicted to anything.

CM: That's understandable, but consider this: A habit that you cannot break is an addiction.

Me: Good point. What can I do to break this addiction?

CM: Witnessing your thoughts was the beginning; you have become aware this is happening. The next step is to understand neuroplasticity. Dispenza said it well: "Neuroplasticity is the change in neural pathways and synapses that occurs due to certain factors, like behavior, environment, or neural processes. During such changes, the brain engages in synaptic pruning, deleting the neural connections that are no longer necessary or useful, and strengthening the necessary ones."

In other words, you can change those neurological pathways and re-wire your brain. When you change a habit successfully, that is what you are doing.

Me: If depression runs in my family, doesn't that mean I will be more likely to experience depression?

CM: That's what people have been taught to believe. But scientists have discovered that with very few exceptions, that isn't true.

Bruce Lipton, in his book Biology of Belief, summarizes, "We are not biological automatons controlled by genes where all of our programs are manifest at the moment of conception and the rest of our life is just playing out the programs of the genes. This is not true at all. That we are dynamic individuals, that we live in the world and biological organisms are capable of adapting to almost any kind of environment. The reason why they are capable of adapting is they are not genetically programmed. That the programs of the genes can change and be modified by the experiences of the individual and the experiences offered by the environment. That through the perception of the living organism, the perception can adjust the biology."

Me: Ok, I think I get it. I'm addicted to depression and all the emotions associated with it.

CM: Yes, but just like the voice in your head is not you, your addiction to depression and the associated emotions are not you either. You are not your body. I know—let it sink in, because what's next will blow your mind.

Me: I'm ready.

CM: You have the power to change your biology, to fire and wire new neurological networks, to rewire your brain, to change your whole life. I liked what Lipton had to say when he discovered this: "The new realization exhilarated me that I could change the character of my life by changing my beliefs. I felt instantly energized because I realized that there was a science-based path that would take me from my job as a perennial 'victim' to my new position as a 'co-creator' of my destiny."

Me: Where do I start?

CM: You become aware of your beliefs and especially your unconscious beliefs. Our beliefs and the thoughts and feelings generated by them offer positive or negative information to our cells. These beliefs run our lives and continue to influence how our cells are reproduced and therefore determine your future experiences. If you stay in your head, you will continue to wire and fire the same neurological connections and continue to reproduce cells with the same signature and signal the same genes. Your work now is to learn how to get out of your head and into your heart. Find the root cause of the negative feeling—the belief behind the feeling. Then let it go, and rewrite the program. Replace that belief with one that serves you.

Me: How do I do this?

CM: There are several tools you can use to do this, but I recommend you meditate.

Me: Meditate! I've been trying that for years.

CM: Yes, but you were probably doing it to relax, to quiet your mind. And that is a good start, but the real power of mediation is to rewire your brain.

Dispenza said: "Meditating is also a means for you to move beyond your analytical mind so that you can access your subconscious mind. That's crucial, since the subconscious is where all your bad habits and behaviors that you want to change reside."

Me: I'm not sure I understand the subconscious mind versus the conscious mind.

CM: Think of your subconscious mind as an unquestioning servant to the conscious mind that works day and night. It stores your beliefs, your previous experiences, your memories, your skills. Everything you have seen, done, or thought is there. The subconscious mind does not have an original thought and accepts what the conscious mind feels to be true. The subconscious will express the feeling that has been impressed upon it without fail. It never tries to alter any belief; it just expresses them in complete detail.

Me: I'm still not sure I fully understand.

CM: Think again about training your players to run a specific play. After many repetitions, the memory of it moved into their subconscious. In contrast, when learning something for the first time, your conscious mind is running the show. In that moment, you are fully conscious—in other words, you are fully aware. But most of the things you do every day you've done hundreds or thousands of times, so that your conscious mind is napping. In fact, it only engages about 5 percent of the time. If this alarms you a little, it should.

Me: So, 95 percent of my waking hours, I'm on autopilot?

CM: Pretty much. It's not a bad thing if the programs you are running keep you safe or serve your higher purpose. If the programs (habits and behaviors) support a healthier, happier you, that's good. It's the bad habits and behaviors, programmed from childhood, that have to be replaced.

Lipton explains it like this: "The fundamental behaviors, beliefs, and attitudes we observe in our parents become 'hardwired' as synaptic pathways in our subconscious minds. Once programmed into the subconscious mind, they control our biology for the rest of our lives ... or at least until we make the effort to reprogram them."

Me: Becoming fully aware seems like a daunting task.

CM: It will take some time and dedication on your part. It isn't easy.

I started to meditate with the intention of pruning old, unhelpful neural pathways and priming new ones. To change my beliefs. I progressed from guided meditations to sitting in silence. I became more aware. I woke up to the fact that our experiences are continually programming us. With every show we watch on TV, every song we hear on the radio, we are programming our unconscious minds. So, despite my progress and the peace I was finding through mediation, I saw that as soon as I left my meditation space and was back in the world, I would be triggered. There was something deeper I wasn't getting.

Me: How do we uncover what we can't get to with our conscious mind? What is going on beneath the surface?

CM: You've hit the shadow. Sooner or later, everyone does.

Me: The shadow?

CM: Shadows are the myths, messages, and beliefs that keep us separated from our sense of wholeness and innate worth. Most of these beliefs are adopted in our early developmental years and reinforced throughout our lives. They manifest themselves as our biases, preferences, and judgments. If we don't learn to integrate the shadow, we will be continuously tripped up by the same limiting unconscious beliefs.

Carl Jung said, "We carry our past with us, to wit, the primitive and inferior man with his desires and emotions, and it is only with an enormous effort that we can detach ourselves from this burden. If it comes to a neurosis, we invariably have to deal with a considerable intensified shadow. And if such a person wants to be cured it is necessary to find a way in which his conscious personality and his shadow can live together."

Me: How do I do this work?

CM: There are several methods available, some better than others. You will need to find what works best for you and approach the work with courage, love, and compassion.

By doing this work, you will not only remove your current blocks but prevent future ones from appearing. It is not only possible to reprogram yourself but also to heal yourself. It is hard work. But if you are brave enough to investigate your psyche and embrace what you see, then your world will never be the same.

Me: Where does this end?

CM: It doesn't end; there is no destination. You've had a moment of awakening, but the work must continue. Don't go back to sleep and leave your life to chance. We are wired to forget; to stay on the path of awakening, you must be a seeker. Take full responsibility for everything in your life. Seek the challenge or the challenge will find you. It is your choice.

Me: What is next?

CM: This is a path of remembering who you truly are and staying connected to that truth. I suggest you continue to find mentorship and proceed on this path of self-realization with a fully integrated approach. Strive to learn what you are studying to be able to teach it. It is only when you can teach that you fully understand and integrate knowledge and experience.

RESOURCES:

Bruce R. Lipton, The Biology of Belief: Unleashing the Power of Consciousness, Matter, & Miracles.

David R. Hawkins, Letting Go: The Pathway of Surrender.

Dr. Joe Dispenza, Breaking The Habit of Being Yourself: How to Lose Your Mind and Create a New One.

Michael A. Singer, The Untethered Soul: The Journey Beyond Yourself.

PRINCIPLES OF TRANSFORMATION

I am fascinated by the process of transformation. This journey we call life has so much to offer if we take the time to look at what the experience in the present moment is trying to show us. These are the principles that guided me from a life of complete despair to feeling that anything is possible and discovering aspects of myself and ways to experience love, joy, and peace that I never thought possible.

Mental freedom is the goal: freedom from guilt, anxiety, doubt, self-judgment, and other's expectations. Going through a day without being controlled by our thoughts. We are creating space between ourselves and what we are experiencing. Space to truly be who we want to be.

I'm going to share with you each of the principles that have provided me a path toward freedom:

- Awareness
- Focus on You First
- Embrace Change
- Life Is a Practice
- Try it On
- Incremental Shifts
- Letting Go and Surrender
- Feeling is the Secret

AWARENESS

"With awareness reality shifts" – Don Miguel Riuz

When we become conscious of our thoughts, feelings, actions, and behaviors, we are developing the critical skill of awareness. When we come to know why we think and feel the way we do, why we get triggered by certain circumstances, and why we seem to hit the same wall every time we try to make a change, we are developing awareness. We are awakening.

There are many types of awareness. What we are speaking about here is self-awareness. There are two types of self-awareness to develop. One is conceptual self-awareness, which is what we think about ourselves—our judgments. The other is embodied self-awareness, which is being able to identify our inner states—what we think and feel. It is quite simple: What we believe and feel will determine our actions, which in turn create our results.

We talked about the relationship between the conscious and subconscious mind. I'm not sure about you, but the more I learn about the power of the subconscious mind, the more I want to wake up and harness its power. Ninety-five percent or more of our thoughts, feelings, and therefore actions are running like a computer program. To put this into perspective, this means that out of 10 minutes randomly selected from our day, we are conscious for less than 30 seconds. If we are awake 16 hours a day, that would mean we are consciously aware for about 45 minutes a day. Ok, what does that mean for you and me? For me, I wanted to know what is going on the other 15 plus hours without me knowing. How awake are you really? I have come to understand that the more I wake up, the more I realize how much I am still asleep.

As we grow up, whether we realize it or not, we are creating our personality. We are choosing what we make each experience mean about ourselves. We are continually creating ourselves and therefore making meaning of the world around us and creating our personal reality. All of this is happening underneath our conscious awareness. This meaning-making is what keeps us from showing up as the best version of ourselves. To change this, we need to take full responsibility for the information that has been programmed into our subconscious mind, become aware of everything we are consuming. Every image from TV to song lyrics makes an impression on our minds. In each moment, our minds are being molded and programmed. We get to decide how our brains are being molded. The information you give your attention to and the unconsciously programmed loops you allow to run, will, as a result, dictate your life experience.

With improved awareness, we can develop the crucial skill of metacognition. Metacognition is learning how to think about our thinking. To examine what thoughts are running our life. Once we become aware, then we can look at our daily habits, thoughts, routines, and unconscious parts of ourselves and determine if they are serving the highest version of ourselves or not. This is where we begin to realize how much opportunity there is for growth. To start choosing a different story and suggesting to ourselves which story we want to live out, we need to utilize the power of awareness as the path to action.

The story that you've told yourself has got you here, now what story will you need to tell yourself to get where you want to go?

FOCUS ON YOU FIRST

The answer to all our problems always comes from within.

When Heidi and I were at a place where we were literally out of answers for each other and felt that we had tried almost everything, we opted for some significant changes. We sold our newly built home and downsized to a lower-maintenance one closer to Heidi's workplace. We got in the best shape of our lives. We worked on our marriage in couples therapy. I left spartan racing and personal training. We tried to simplify our lives in any way we could.

Those changes helped, but we were both still unhappy. One evening, we found ourselves on opposite sides of the kitchen island having the most real conversation we'd ever had. It was about the finality of our marriage. "Should I move out? Have we tried everything?"

In a state of complete despair and disbelief, I had a download of clarity. We were focusing on the wrong things. We were trying to change everything outside of ourselves, and even each other. I suggested we live like roommates for the next six months. We would focus entirely on ourselves—our separate growth and healing journeys. We would be selfish with our time and energy. Then we'll come back and discuss what our future holds. If we truly do the work on ourselves and grow further apart, then that's what is meant to happen. Our only chance to grow back together is to find what we need within ourselves first. As we did the work, we ended up naturally falling back in love and growing even closer in the process.

The number one motivation to transform needs to be you. It's easier to say, I want to change for my kids or loved ones, or, I want to make my parents proud. The truth is, it needs to be about you. The only way to show up fully for our world is to study yourself, know yourself, and become more whole by integrating all parts of yourself. How you treat yourself is how you will treat others. The more love, patience, compassion you can show yourself, the more you will be able to give the same to others. To grow, we need to set up our environment for growth, and the essential environment that needs tending is internal. Take full responsibility for who you are being by looking inward.

As we look inward and do the work on ourselves, we quiet our minds and get in touch with deeper aspects of ourselves. We begin to recognize the source of our motivation. My initial motivation began with relieving pain and suffering and wanting to break the cycle of depression that was starting to show up in my son. As the work evolved, the motivation shifted toward mastery in service to others. The more I can show up fully for myself, the more I can positively impact my family and community. In this process of focusing inward, I noticed a profound shift from running away from pain to chasing hope and light.

Self-evaluation is key. Take a look at all the roles you play—husband/wife, father/mother, brother/sister, friend. Ask yourself, how am I showing up in these roles? Where am I missing the mark? It is crucial to look at the most important relationship we're in—the one we have with ourselves. How do I treat myself physically, mentally, emotionally? As we evaluate ourselves in the different roles we play, we will be given opportunities to see who it is we are being. Take the time in these moments to ponder and ask yourself, if I was being the best version of myself? What would that look like, how would that feel, what habits would I have, what kind of thoughts would be running in my head? What is the gap between who I am being and the best version of myself? Develop the skill of self-study. I see room for improvement in every aspect of my life every day. How can I be a better listener as a husband, be more present as a father, be more curious as a friend, be more empathetic as a neighbor, believe in myself more?

It always starts by looking inward to find our purpose and what we stand for.

EMBRACE CHANGE

"The secret of change is to focus all of your energy not on fighting the old, but building the new." – Socrates

I remember my college head coach, John Zamberlin, speaking this basic truth almost every day during stretching sessions before practice. He would yell out in his booming voice, "We are either getting better or we are getting worse, there ain't no staying the same."

Change is inevitable. It is an absolute truth of life. It is natural for everything to be changing and evolving continually. Our cells are reproducing at an incredible rate of 50–70 billion cells each day. Cell reproduction is change happening in every moment. With this in mind, we are not the same person as yesterday or even five minutes ago. We must accept and allow change, flow with it without clinging to the past. Once we accept that everything is continually changing, we unlock our potential to be more present with what is happening right now. It is our resistance to change that ultimately leads to suffering. How many times do you have conversations that start with could have, should have or would have? If we are living in the past, we are avoiding the next evolution of ourselves and not allowing change to happen.

As we begin to allow and cultivate change in our lives, we can almost always expect change to be met with resistance. This resistance shows up due to the process of change. Breaking old neurological pathways and replacing them with new ones, reprogramming cells, breaking the chemical addictions of the past and teaching the body how to feel it's way into the future. This resistance is the sign that you are in the middle of the river of change. This is when change can also be exciting; it is what leads us to the next adventure, the next experience of our life.

The more we embrace change, the more we tend to be excited to see what is going to happen next. We adopt a different role in creating our future, and we become comfortable with being uncomfortable; we find joy in new experiences.

We look forward to how changes will bring more opportunities for growth and abundance. Embrace change and become a seeker of challenges rather than waiting for the challenge to come to you.

When I started this journey, I desperately wanted to know what it would look like. I had no idea what was in store for me—what my obstacles would be, what my victories would be, in what ways I would have to redirect, how my relationships would change. How would the vision I held for my life change?

Embrace your story by first accepting where you are. You can change anything and everything from there. There's power in knowing that what you choose to do now will impact where you end up. We can be whoever we desire to be and create habits, rituals, routines that will build the story that we want to live.

Whether we choose to embrace it or not, we're either growing or we're dying—there ain't no staying the same.

LIFE IS A PRACTICE

A day without intention is a day left to chance.

I'm amazed by how each moment in life offers us an opportunity to practice. I like to look at life as a game and each moment as our practice field. Would you take a football team into a game day without practicing? No. There is so much preparation for those few game days each year. If you were to add up the amount of time spent practicing, each coach and player spends the majority of their year preparing for game day. So that when we get to the big game, everybody shows up as the best player and coaches they can be, to win! That is true in life as well. Life is a game, and we need to practice to win on the game field of life. A foundational principle of Mark Divine's Unbeatable Mind program is

"First, we must win in our Minds." So much can be done to win in our mind before we ever set foot on the game field of life. We start our day with intention and visualization, so that as the unpredictable happens on game day, we can make adjustments and believe in ourselves during moments of adversity.

Early in my meditative practice, I was all about chasing the mystical experience. I was obsessed with how I could take myself to a place of bliss. I could go to that place of bliss whenever I wanted. But this sense of peace disappeared as soon as the session ended and I was back in the 3D world. It honestly was depressing. I thought to myself, What's the point? I just wanted to stay there, blissed out, and avoid the real world. There were multiple times deep in meditation that I resisted returning to my life as husband, father, business owner, etc.

One of my mentors informed me that the point of meditation isn't to go there and escape our problems, but to experience a deep knowing of love and peace and bring it back with us. So, we can walk around with this experience in our hearts and share it with those we love the most. We practice developing the witness, the ability to separate ourselves from our thoughts and emotions. In doing so, we realize that we are not our thoughts; we are the ones watching our thoughts. We are not our emotions; we are the ones experiencing our emotions. As I was able to embrace this concept of life being a practice, I noticed that my sense of wholeness and peace would stay with me longer throughout the day. My practice went from being an escape from life to a way of life.

I used to try hard to rid myself of any negative self-talk. I would beat myself up for relaxing, too, even for just a minute. The harder I tried to get rid of the negative thoughts in my head, the more exhausting it was. The more I resisted them, the more energy they seemed to take. Have you ever heard the saying, "What we resist, persists"? It wasn't until I was able to just watch what was going on in my head that I could truly begin to make sense of my experience. Like clouds passing over a mountain, here comes a thought, and there it goes—with no label attached, good or bad. Everything is there to experience and learn from. I began to continually bring myself back to the present moment to allow myself to choose the next experience consciously. That is the practice.

Moment by moment, we are given the opportunity to either show up as the best version of ourselves or fall into the trap of the illusions going on in our heads. Life as a practice means we commit to it every day. We practice with earnestness by setting intentions in alignment with who we came here to be. It means we commit to a practice for the rest of our lives as if we are preparing for something, because we are. Yes, this practice is FOREVER!

If you are not committing to a lifetime of practice, then you might as well wait and start when you are ready.

TRY IT ON

We don't know what we don't know.

In order to transform, we need to try new things. We must be curious and open. The try it on principle is one that I adopted when I realized I didn't have all the answers, and the way I was going about things wasn't working. It is simple: If you do not like the results you're getting, then something you are doing, who you are being, or what you are thinking needs to change.

I used to get frustrated when I coached incoming freshmen who thought they knew it all. One of the biggest lessons for young athletes coming in is to find out they don't know shit. In high school, they may have been team captain, all-state, and the hero of their hometown, but in college they are just another fish in a bigger pond. Anyone who plays Division I football was probably the best player on their high school team. Some players struggle to let go of their ego and it holds them back from improvement. The players that develop the fastest and reach their potential are the ones who allow themselves to be coached.

The more I learn, the more I realize how much I don't know. When I truly became ready for change, I was willing to try anything. I wanted to know what was working for other people. What thoughts and beliefs did they have, how did they go about their day, how did they start their day, what tools did they have? If it was working for them, maybe it would work for me as well.

How are we supposed to know if something works for us unless we have our own experience of it? It reminds me of getting my two young kids to eat certain foods at the dinner table. They see something that to them looks weird or gross, and they decide they don't like it. The other day I made a meatloaf grilled cheese sandwich—let me tell you, it was delicious. Both my kids looked at it and said, "Ewww, gross." I convinced them to try it by taking a huge bite out of it and thoroughly make a show of enjoying it. They decided to give it a try—and of course, they loved it! If they never tried it, they would have missed out on the experience and wouldn't have realized that melted cheese over meat-loaf is delicious.

How many things do we decide not to try because they are new or dif-ferent? We often skip trying something new because it argues with our current sense of reality or belief structure. What if giving a new thought, concept, idea, exercise, or tool a try is the next dot that needs to be connected for you to evolve to the next version of yourself? How does this work? It's simple, it is no different than trying on a new jacket. Does the jacket fit? Do you like the color? Are the pockets in the right place? How does it feel? Is it the right size? Will it be warm enough? Does it suit your purpose? This applies to thoughts, beliefs, principles, values, tools, exercises, even future visualizations of yourself. Try them on, see how they fit, how they feel, give yourself the experience of something new so you can decide for yourself.

What do you have to lose? Be open and curious.

Try it on!

INCREMENTAL SHIFTS

What once seemed like insane discipline soon becomes a way of life.

Transformation is a process. Wouldn't it be exciting if we woke up one day and everything had magically changed? In my experience, transfor-mation doesn't work that way. There's much to learn on this journey we call life, and making lasting changes takes time and patience. In the past, I'd try making too many changes at once and meet all kinds of resistance, most of it internal. I once tried going from not working out to doing two hours a day, six days a week—and wondered after two weeks why it didn't stick. In contrast, if we take on small incremental changes daily and see them as small victories over time, they add up to a massive transformation. New Year's resolutions fail because they are too drastic. Conversely, small adjustments can lead to real change .

I am tired of people in the personal growth world telling people they can take their 10-year goals and turn them into 6-month goals. Ironically, these same people don't have families and are out of touch with where transformation starts. These claims can market a book or program and may work for a few, but for the rest of us common humans with complicated lives, it won't work and will do more harm than good.

Naturally, as we continue to expand our capacity for growth, we can take on more. When we're getting started, though, we should take things on one at a time. Otherwise, there is a strong tendency to quit. We need to set ourselves up for success by setting small, achievable goals daily, then celebrating the wins along the way. This creates momentum and helps us form habits that serve our highest good.

In implementing an incremental approach to personal development we can rely on a very simple rule—never go more than 48 hours without doing the daily practices that help you stay connected with your purpose and remind you of who you have come here to be. If you fall off your routine—the practice (that keeps you in the flow)— then pick yourself right back up and continue to do the work. Soon you will find that what once seemed like insane discipline will become a way of life. Discipline is a skill just like anything else; it can be developed through small incremental steps.

My personal belief is that failure is not necessary; it is all a matter of perspective. I look at my life and notice a lot of mistakes along with things that I consider to be divine redirection, but failure is something that we expose ourselves to by choice. If I call it a failure, then that is what it becomes. If I call it a divine redirection or lesson learned, then that is what it becomes. What message do you want your unconscious mind to take on about yourself? My little secret—you do not have to fail to succeed. You do have to take on things one at a time as they come, and no matter what, keep going.

Commit to making incremental progress and getting just 1 percent better every day; one incremental shift at a time.

LETTING GO AND SURRENDER
"The price of the new life is the old one" - unknown

Preferences. We all have them, but what are yours potentially costing you? I believe our preferences are what stand between us and everything we want. They are the wall between our loved ones and us, between our current marriage and the marriage that's possible for us, between our existing relationship with our kids and the desired one. Preferences are layers of ego that separate us from our true selves and everything we want in life. Most of the time, our preferences are unconscious—we are not aware of them.

Our preferences determine our path. As we navigate life, we pick up preferences along the way. Some of my small ones include: I like it quiet when I'm drinking my coffee in the morning, I hate dishes in the sink, I like a clean car. I also like dinner at a certain time and the house at a specific temp. And by the way, if I'm drinking a latte, I want it crafted to perfection. You get the picture. With every new preference, however, we sacrifice mental freedom. We limit our opportunities to get where we're going and limit further what it will look like when we get there.

If we are not aware of this constant accumulation of preferences, it can be like being stuck on the freeway in gridlock traffic, with all exits closed due to construction. As we let go of our preferences, options begin to open up. The construction crew finishes and the exits open to new possibilities. We find a better and easier way to get where we're going.

It takes strength to let go of preferences that keep getting in our way so we can focus our attention on what truly matters. Last year my entire extended family took a week-long vacation in Hawaii. This included my wife and kids and also both of my brothers and their kids, along with my parents. There were 12 of us in the house for over a week. In the first few minutes of the first day, I was trying to read my book, poolside, when the chaos began. I quickly realized I was experiencing irritation and annoyance with everybody because we all had different preferences and expectations for the day and each other. At that moment, I decided to experiment. For the entire week, I was going to let go of all my preferences. Every time I found myself wanting to do something different than what was being asked of me, I let go of my preference and did whatever the other person wanted. For example, every time my kids said, "Dad, will you swim with me?" I replied, "Yes!" I found that every time I let go of my preferences, I was able to connect with my loved ones more deeply and I found so much peace in letting go. At the end of the week we were having dinner on the beach, and Heidi turned to me and said, "Ryan you look like a man that doesn't have any preferences, you seem so peaceful." I laughed.

Letting go of your preferences is a practice of presence; it allows you to be in the present moment fully without wanting something to be different. Surrendering is the act of releasing something, releasing your grip on your identity, your ego, your attachment to thoughts and feelings. I know what you are thinking—Surrender? fuck that, I don't surrender to shit! This was the mentality I once had. Surrender meant weakness. In this context, surrender doesn't mean to give up or quit. Surrender is potentially the single hardest and most important part of transformation. Surrender is a path that allows for possibility, and it allows us to let go of the old stories that keep us stuck in the same current existence. It allows us to find who we truly are at the core and develop a stronger sense of self.

The sooner we surrender our ego, the faster we are able to develop and grow. The more we learn and get ourselves out of the way, the more accelerated our development becomes.

A few years ago, I went on a camping trip with a handful of my best college buddies. It was assumed when we all got together we'd have a few too many cocktails and reminisce about the good old days. At the time, I was deep into doing the work and was committed to maintaining an agreement with myself not to drink. I wanted to experience that weekend differently—to have a good time being around the friends who fired up those old neurological pathways but without acting on the urge to partake in the drinking. As the weekend progressed and everybody got the message that I woudn't budge, I ended up having a great time. We ate like kings, built a huge fire, shot some guns, and had a typical guys' weekend.

The interesting part was on the way home. At first, I felt incredibly proud of myself. I did it! I proved to myself that I was in control. I was able to be in that environment, and this new version of myself over-came the old conditioning. Then the old program of depression hit, and it hit hard. It lasted almost a full five days, and it was brutal. I wrote a journal entry about my experience at the time.

Journal Entry:

It is dark and lonely. It is impossible to enjoy the little things like playing with your kids or talking with your wife because you can't keep your mind in the present moment. When you think about doing the things that you know will help you, such as meditation, exercise, breathing, writing ... you don't have the energy or focus to be able to go through with it—in fact, your body tells you to stop because it will be too painful. It is impossible to even see into the next moment. I can't see anything in the future. I cannot even see to the end of the day or waking up tomorrow, much less dream or cast a vision of hope. My eyes feel heavy, my shoulders hunch over, and I feel I am on the verge of tears. There is a tightness in my throat like I may choke if tried to eat. I am not worthy of anything. My happiness is not important. I just hope and pray that I don't project this feeling onto the ones I love most, so I try to hide it. I pretend like everything is fine or ok. I curl up into a ball and want to hide. The world is better off without me. Peace and Joy feel like a pipe dream, and I want to judge anyone else that may show these gifts in their life. I start to look for every reason possible to affirm this is who I am, and this is exactly how I should feel.

This was an opportunity to surrender. As I was experiencing this and writing I was fully aware that it was an old program. I was writing it down to separate myself from the experience I was having. I noticed I was no longer attaching to these old stories and emotions. I just al-lowed the feelings to be there, feeling fully without judgment, not try-ing to change anything. I focused on the energy behind the feeling without resisting it. I didn't engage with thoughts that came up about the feeling but instead consciously released each of them. I felt a shift internally and a calm sense of freedom.

This is the act of surrender, releasing the grip of attachment to old stories and no longer identifying with the depression. I could feel the energy liberating itself inside my body as old parts of me were healing. I used to say, "my depression," "my anxiety," like it was me. Now it is just the experience of the depression. There it is, and here I am. Thoughts are endless; there can be thousands of thoughts surrounding just one feeling. By letting go of one feeling at a time, it's possible to stay in a place of freedom.

You are watching your feelings come and go and realizing you are not those feelings. You are the pure, whole being witnessing them, and you are free.

FEELING IS THE SECRET

"He who is the cause of all life acts through the sense of feeling. You can think of a thousand things, yet not be moved to act upon one of them. A deep conviction—felt, is far more important than anything you could ever think." – Neville Goddard

Can you imagine that you had a secret power your whole life and never realized it? Even worse, what if your secret power was something everybody told you not to use when you were a kid, so you grew up hiding it, suppressing it, avoiding it at all costs, and believing it was terrible. Yes, our feelings are our secret power. Our feelings are there to communicate with something larger than ourselves. Our feelings are there to guide us (intuition). Our feelings are there to let us know something is out of alignment. Our feelings are there to allow us to heal. Our feelings are there like magnets drawing in our future.

David R. Hawkins, in his book titled Letting Go, talks about emotions being energy-in-motion. If we allow for these feelings to fully arise without judgment and without attachment, they will only last 90 seconds. When we don't allow ourselves to fully feel the emotion, it creates blockages. These blockages get our attention eventually by manifesting as physical illnesses or depression and anxiety.

From my current perspective, I'm able to look back at my journey of suffering and realize that the anxiety and depression was there trying to teach me something. If I had slowed down and listened, I could have learned what I needed and wouldn't have suffered like I did. Our feelings are there to communicate with us like a message coming from our future self or higher self to help us right the ship and course-correct.

We can channel our emotions into being a magnet for our future. We can imagine what it would feel like to be our future self and, in doing so, draw ourselves closer to that experience. We can set up the neurological pathways that will develop us into who we desire to be!

Fully feeling our feelings is our gift as human beings. It is the experience of being human. The more we allow ourselves to explore and feel, the more our potential grows and our intuition develops; and we begin to attract our future self and the situations and people into our lives that will serve our highest good.

Are you ready to acknowledge your superpower and get curious about what you are feeling?

RESOURCES:

David R. Hawkins (2014) Letting Go: The Pathway of Surrender

CYCLE OF TRANSFORMATION

Everyone has a unique and personal experience with their transformational journey. And it is probably safe to say that we are all trying to get to the same place. Freedom. Freedom in all aspects of our lives.

I noticed, as I began my journey in earnest, committed and disciplined, that there is a consistent pattern connecting all my experiences. The phases in the model I have created continuously repeat as each new area of growth is presented. The Cycle of Transformation phases act as a road map, helping me stay aware of where I am in relation to my own evolution and growth, in each moment, day, or week. This awareness of where I am in the cycle helps me remember which tools to use, and it establishes trail markers along the way, clearly identifying where I need to sit back to gain perspective or reach out to my coach or mentor for help.

The different stages of the Cycle of Transformation are Choice Point, The Void, The Climb, Plateaus and False Summits, and Integration. My hope is that you use this model to help guide you toward a clearer insight into your transformation as you move from Choice Point through Integration and back to a new Choice Point again.

The Cycle of Transformation:

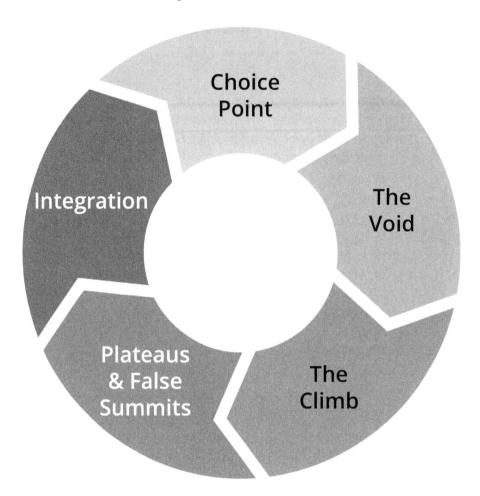

CHOICE POINT

We are either being conditioned into an experience of further suffering or consciously choosing a new experience.

Most transformation begins because we find ourselves in a place of pain or suffering. We must first become aware that we want something different. Feeling like something is missing, realizing the way we are living is not how we intended to live or how we genuinely want to live, is the first step toward transformation. For me, it was a simple thought: Is this it? The thought that there must be something more moved me into exploring what that could be.

Once we determine we are not living the way we desire, it is time to take full responsibility for our choices in each moment. Decisions can be intentional and conscious or habitual and unconscious. Once we choose intentionally to make changes in our lives, the work begins.

As we create this awareness, we begin to awaken to the fact that we have something going on in each moment that we can either attach to or let go of and replace with something that serves us. We recognize that the mental chatter or voice in our head that is always there is an invitation to use the greatest gift of all, CHOICE. We get to choose where our attention goes. Attention is noticing, being aware of, observing, or concentrating on a particular subject or object. Becoming aware of what information we are consuming, moment-by-moment. What loops are running through our heads as recurring thoughts are happening? How are we reacting to our environment and circumstances?

If we feed into negative thoughts and attach to them, we are giving energy to negativity. If we notice and release negative thoughts and replace them with positive thoughts, we are providing power to positivity. Eventually, we can create a positive loop that is running without our conscious effort as well as our reactions to interactions with our environment. If we continue to react the same way every time something happens that argues with our preferences, we will reinforce that preference and reaction to the circumstance. If we can allow our circumstances to be there and yet remain non-reactive then we will be able to prune that old conditioned reaction and replace it with the desired response.

A simple story may help shed some light on my point. I used to have the same experience every time I cleaned up a job site after a day of painting a house. One small task always frustrated me beyond measure: rolling up the extension cords. I had this conditioned experience that rolling up extension cords is irritating. It wasn't whether I'd get triggered, it was just how long it would take. This may sound pathetic, but I believed my personality wasn't meant to roll up extension cords. I was just too impatient. I had plenty of proof of this, because every time I rolled one up, it got knotted or tangled or, god forbid, stuck under the sprayer or around a bush. Finally, I was able to challenge this conditioning by practicing rolling up an extension cord while focusing my attention on presence and ease. It worked: I stopped getting irritated. I now laugh every time I roll up an extension cord because I remember and feel the old conditioning wanting to start, but I choose a different experience.

Other examples of conditioned reactions to our environment or circumstances could be these: getting cut off in traffic, hitting all the red lights, being interrupted in a conversation, finding the house a mess, failing to find the desired clothes to wear. Every time these things happen, and you react in a conditioned way, you are strengthening that conditioning. We do not have to react from these conditioned states. We can choose to respond as our best self rather than allow for conditioned reaction to run our life.

When we become aware of what our attention is on or notice a conditioned reaction, that moment is our CHOICE POINT. The choice is ours. Continue to run the old conditioned reflex or thought loop or pause, breathe, and decide to choose a different response or thought, thus creating a new program. It's not the large choices in life that define us; it's all the small choices accumulated over time. In each moment, we are presented with an opportunity to focus on what we want to experience instead of what we don't want. Where we place our attention is the determining factor in who we become.

Questions for Self-Reflection:

- What is a conditioned response to an everyday circumstance that you can awaken to and challenge?
- What is a negative thought pattern that you can replace with a positive thought?
- What conditioned patterns are you allowing to run that are not serving you?
- Where is your attention right now?

THE VOID

We must clear space, simplify, and declutter our lives to make room to do the work.

The best place to create something new is from nothing or emptiness. But first, we must declutter our life to make room for change. We declutter our minds, our environments, our habits, and maybe most importantly, our circle of influence. When we begin to declutter, we find ourselves in the unknown. In the unknown, life can feel like there is a void as if something is missing. We will instantly notice what I call internal pushback. A sense of loss, a feeling of uncertainty like we should be doing something different. Lots of chatter in our minds. (This is the process of pruning old neurological connections.)

This void feels uncomfortable; therefore, we fill the void with buffering or distractions such as food, alcohol, spending money, watching sports, etc. Buffering is when we do something to avoid the discomfort of the unknown or what we don't want to face and feel. Ironically, in the void is where the magic happens, where we get to make shit up. Rather than filling the void with something that is known, memorized, and comfortable, we can use our imagination to dream up a different version of ourselves. Create new habits, patterns, thoughts, and behaviors that lead to a completely different experience of life.

Here's an example of how creating the void worked for me:

After I left coaching, one of the habits I fell into was being a super fan. At first, I loved watching a good college football game. But before long, I was spending an abundance of time watching whatever game happened to be on. I watched football just to watch football. I thought I loved it, but I realized what I was doing was watching someone else live their dream. It reminded me of something I had learned about mirror neurons: We can watch others achieve an accomplishment and feel the experience as if it is ours. This can be useful if we are tapping into this kind of experience in order to motivate us to take a particular action. But there are two sides to every coin. We may love this vicarious experience, but at the end of the afternoon, and the next one, too, we (and our nachos) haven't left the couch. I'd rather have a new experience. How about you?

After recognizing this, I made a drastic change. I canceled our cable TV, made a commitment not to watch football in our home, and got down to one TV in the basement for the occasional movie with the wife and kids. On the first Saturday of autumn, I found myself pacing around the kitchen, trying to decide how to occupy myself. I was missing out. What amazing plays are happening that I could be watching live?

I observed myself breaking an old habit. I could feel the neurological connections short-circuiting: Where is the black hole I used to stare at for hours? I began to find things I would rather be doing to fill my time: connecting with those I love the most, taking long nature hikes as a family, spending time with my kids doing whatever they wanted, going on camping trips with a group of like-minded men. These things filled me up and made me so much more at peace and grounded.

The initial void was uncomfortable, but I remember one Saturday after a few months I suddenly realized it was 5 o'clock and I hadn't even thought about football or wondered what the scores were. Two years into this new way of life I had even forgotten about Superbowl Sunday. Heidi asked me if I was going to watch the game. "What game are you talking about?" I said.

Sometimes what is enjoyable in the short term can end up leading to suffering later because it is distracting us from the discomfort of the unknown and therefore delaying a new experience of life.

What is hard in the short term can lead to more peace, joy, and clarity of purpose in the long haul.

Questions for Self-Reflection:

- What is something you can remove from your life to make room for the unknown?
- What is something you are holding on to that you are ready to let go of?
- What habits are sabotaging your potential?
- Who can you spend less time with to be more in alignment with who you are becoming?
- Who can you spend more time with to gain more support for who you are becoming?

THE CLIMB

Fall in love with the process.

This is where most people quit. This is where it goes from knowledge to experience. This is where the rubber meets the road, and we start truly unpacking what's going on. We start laying down the framework for our future experiences. There is no way I would be able to describe all the aspects of doing the work, and even if I did, your experience will be unique to your journey.

What I can tell you is doing the work is like being in the jungle with a machete hacking away trying to create a new road out of nothing, and you aren't even sure where you are going. And just in view there is a four-lane highway where everybody else is traveling in cars with AC and drinking a latte. As you continue to hack away at the jungle, what motivates you to keep swinging that machete is knowing you can't go back.

Doing the work means taking on a fully integrated approach to life. You must be willing to pick up a book, try an exercise, adopt a tool, and create your own experience to actually have lasting change.

It's essential to take an integrated approach to assess and grow yourself across the three pillars of self-development: physical, mental, and emotional. Building the disciplines into your life such as morning routines; studying new topics; challenging your beliefs; merging your gut, heart, and mind to develop more profound intuition; and finding your sense of purpose are pivotal for your evolution. Using the tools and practices that support your development in each of these pillars unlocks your full potential to transform and change your life.

The work requires truly becoming a student of life. I used to be guilty of reading a book and then simply telling people, "That was a good book." If someone asked me what made it useful, I would be able to give them a brief overview of the book, but that would be about it. I was just reading for information. When a book has questions that relate to the topic you are studying, stop and answer those questions before continuing with the book. Reading a book with a notepad and highlighter has an entirely different engagement than leisurely listening to an audiobook on the way to work. Action and application and eventually integration lead to wisdom, which leads to new experiences, which leads to new opportunities, which leads to a new life. Information is not meant to stay on the page; it is intended to be turned into wisdom. The only way to turn information into wisdom through experience is to do the work.

I've had many moments where I wished I never embarked on this journey of self-improvement. But just on the other side of those moments of frustration was a more in-depth knowledge that allowed me to connect the dots that pointed me in the right direction. This is why it is so essential to find mentorship and coaching to help you stay on track. Most of the time, it is challenging to see our BOO (background of obviousness). BOO is an Unbeatable Mind term that points to our shadow or deep-seated belief systems embedded from past experiences, cultural and societal biases, language, and family. It is of great benefit to have someone on your side, helping you identify your BOO, looking out for pitfalls and rabbit holes thrown up by your subconscious mind.

If you are old enough to remember what it was like before GPS or can imagine that you couldn't use your phone to lookup an address, think about how long it would take you to stop and ask for directions. Or would you potentially be the one to give up before you ask? How much easier would it be if we stopped and asked for help? How much energy and time could you have saved? Most importantly, how much quicker will we get where we want to go if we ask someone who knows how to get there or can at least point us in the right direction.

It is imperative during the Climb that we take an integrated approach, become a student of life, ask for help, find mentorship, hire a coach, and accept that we cannot do it alone. There isn't a step-by-step playbook on how to navigate life. We depend on those that have walked the path before us to illuminate the path, so we don't have to make the same mistakes they did.

We should always be learning from someone that exhibits the qualities we aspire to cultivate. They can help us ensure that we are walking the right path.

Questions for Self-Reflection:

- Who can you reach out to for mentorship?
- What practice can you take on right now to create a shift in your life?
- What are you ignoring or suppressing within yourself that is ready to be seen?
- What challenges can you face that you have been avoiding?

PLATEAUS AND FALSE SUMMITS
"There is no there, there" - Gertrude Stein

The pursuit of self-mastery doesn't mean we'll become masters; it means we're committed to being warriors on the battlefield of life. We will continue to do the work that is necessary to reach our highest potential. Each Mountain we climb in pursuit of this potential has vantage points where we can recognize through experience that we have transcended an earlier version of ourselves. As we climb the mountains of human development, we will experience plateaus. We notice a shift in consciousness; we become more aware, we experience new levels of peace, joy, and abundance. Maybe achieve a specific goal or desired outcome. When we cross these thresholds, we tend to think we have made it to a particular destination. We find ourselves wanting to stop and take a look around. Rightfully so, we should take a moment and acknowledge our progress.

I remember early in my transformation having moments of clarity and relief; I believed that I had made it. I would think to myself: I won. What now? At the time, I didn't realize that this is the never-ending story: No matter how much work we do, there will always be more. I would let my guard down, slowing down the practices that kept me growing, but it wasn't long before I realized that the perceived summit was a false summit; there was no real summit in sight. I learned to accept the truth that there truly is no there, there. With this realization, my practices took on new meaning. There was a release of control; I was no longer grasping at the idea of "arriving." I developed a new mindset that self-mastery meant to continue to climb each mountain out of curiosity of what the next view or perspective would be without attachment to staying in any one place for long. It became about the journey.

We are creatures of growth, and when we reach these plateaus, it is a time for reflection and acknowledgment of progress. Next, we take the opportunity to recalibrate, refocus, and set the next course of action. Decide on our next challenge, set our next intention, learn a new skill, go deeper into our practices, revisit and refine our craft of mastering ourselves. Because of the nature of the mind, we will never be on firm ground. If we try to stay at a particular plateau for too long, the earth will slip out from underneath our feet, but slow enough that we might not notice it.

Another challenge of the Climb is that each new reference point of our growth is the last plateau. This can create a sense of lack because it is easy to forget how far we've come; we tend only to see where we are and where we aren't. This new perspective of growth is what I call the new baseline. Even though we are showing up in our life operating from this new baseline, all we see is how far we must climb to the next false summit. To meet this challenge, we just need to continue the climb and focus on the moment, enjoying every step along the way. Something is freeing about not trying to be any particular place other than exactly where you are, and knowing you'd better enjoy this place because you will soon be moving on.

As we experience more of these plateaus, we begin to take ourselves a little less seriously and find enjoyment in the unknown; we become seekers of challenges. We are always looking to where we can grow because we know that with growth comes a new experience and another reminder that all we truly have is right here and right now. So, enjoy it, all of it.

Question for Self-Reflection:

- What accomplishments can you acknowledge within your journey?
- What are you proud of yourself for?
- How can you get back on track in your life?
- What's next?

INTEGRATION

Real transformation is when you realize you can't go back to the old patterns, beliefs, and way of life.

This is where it gets fun; we go from doing to being. We have fully integrated a new way of thinking, a new way of being into our lives. We go from doing the practices to being the practices. We realize that we created the version of ourselves that gets up to do the morning routine because that's just what we do. We take all the authentic actions as our future self and get to observe ourselves, showing up that way for ourselves and others.

My family and I were up at Priest Lake for the weekend, and on Sunday morning I woke up and checked my weather app. I like to watch the sunrise on clear mornings from Indian Rock, where I've gone for years. Colton, my son, loves to join me for sunrises as well. So, we hopped up and went together.

We headed out to Indian Rock almost an hour before sunrise, so we had some time to practice. I did some box breathing with Colton. Then he sat patiently as I went into a Qi Gong stance. I was meditating, cultivating energy and gratitude, and grounding through my bare feet when I had a flashback into the past. I did a recapitulation of my spiritual journey, of my evolution, of my personal development, and I had this realization:

I have been doing meditation for a clear mind. I have been working out to achieve a leaner, stronger body. I realized I still had ulterior motives. I was meditating to relieve suffering, to quiet the mind; I always wanted something in return. And in that moment, on that rock, in my standing meditation, I witnessed a thought—When is this sun ever going to come up? Then the thought, I don't give a shit how long it takes for the sun to come up. I'm just grateful for the time to practice with my son. I'm going to stand here in this stance, my arms out in a circle like I'm holding onto a ball, and watch these thoughts pass by. I smiled, realizing that I'm doing this because I enjoy the shit out of it. I'm doing this because I like to feel connected. I'm doing this because I genuinely want to practice. I am no longer doing this; I am being this, and being the practice is the practice.

This is integration when we become what we practice. We become the one watching us practice; there is a merge of our future self and current self. This is such a gift to ourselves and those around us. We genuinely have transformed into a better version of ourselves, and everybody around us benefits from it. We realize that transformation has happened, and there is no going back to the old experience. The really fun part is when people, opportunities, and signs show up because of who you are being. As we continue to operate from this authentic place, we feel whole and connected. We then find the next choice point and continue the climb.

Questions for Self-Reflection:

- What authentic action can you take to show up fully for yourself?
- What part of yourself can you acknowledge to become the highest expression of yourself?
- What truth about yourself are you ignoring or hiding?
- How can you step into your power?

GETTING STARTED

My goal for this section of the book is to give you a starting point and references to go deeper. In it, I describe the foundational tools and practices that started me on my journey and continued work; I believe they will work for you as well if you approach these practices with consistency, curiosity, and commitment. The only way for you to truly understand how powerful these tools and practices are is to have your own experience.

The path to freedom has been illuminated by all who have walked it before us. It is up to you to walk your own path. Without practice, nothing will change. I encourage you to practice daily, with an open mind and an open heart, allowing yourself to be with each experience fully without judgment. Commit to this path of self-realization and you will create trail markers along the way that will allow you to remember who you are and who you have come here to be.

Except for tools and practices that I have developed myself, I do not go into great detail as there are far better references that I will point you to, should you want to explore further.

Feel free to jump around and find the practice that resonates with you. Remember, this is your practice, and each individual will find some tools more impactful than others. It is crucial to understand that the idea of practice has two parts to it. It is finding the personal balance between intention and surrender. Be very intentional in your practice every day, but understand that once you've done the work and planted the seed, you must let go of outcomes and be present in the moment. Finding this balance is an art that each of us needs to pursue and be mindful of.

As we practice with intention, we accelerate our growth so we can serve others and the good of the world.

Before you begin to use the tools and practices, I recommend you start with these exercises.

- Self-Assessment
- Defining Success
- Setting Intentions
- Setting your Minimums
- Finding Mentorship

SELF-ASSESSMENT

This is where it all begins. Determining where we are in life and who we are being in the different roles and categories of life. Consider who you might be if you were the best version of yourself and identify the gap between the two. Find the largest gaps and begin to close them by doing the work.

Try it on!

Self-Assessment Exercise:

Rate yourself on a scale of 1–5 by circling one of the numbers below each of the following questions:

1 Never

2 Sometimes

3 About half the time

4 Most of the time

5 All of the time

Physical:

Are you comfortable in your body?

1 2 3 4 5

Do you feel strong and flexible?

1 2 3 4 5

Do you have a balanced nutritional plan?

1 2 3 4 5

Do your sleep habits fit your life goals?

1 2 3 4 5

Do you have Sustained energy throughout the day?

1 2 3 4 5

Mental:

Do you work to expand your mental capacity?

1 2 3 4 5

Do you respond well to stress?

1 2 3 4 5

Is it easy for you to make decisions?

1 2 3 4 5

Do you find the positive in all situations?

1 2 3 4 5

Do you tend to give up easily?

1 2 3 4 5

Emotional:

Do your emotions influence your decisions?

1 2 3 4 5

Do you express your emotions in a healthy manner?

1 2 3 4 5

Are you a good listener?

1 2 3 4 5

Are you aware of the cause of negative emotions?

1 2 3 4 5

Are you able to reflect upon negative emotions?

1 2 3 4 5

Are you able to shift your emotional state?

1 2 3 4 5

Are you able to let things go?

1 2 3 4 5

Are you comfortable talking about your emotions?

1 2 3 4 5

Do you have healthy relationships?

1 2 3 4 5

DEFINING SUCCESS

It is crucial that you clearly define what success means to you. By defining success, you will be able to set clear expectations for yourself. Make sure that the expectations you set and how you define success is not coming from your environment, society, and background. We get to decide what expectations we are going to live up to. Sit with this question, ponder it, and have patience in finding the answer. Be prepared for your answer to change over time; this is normal. I used to define success in a completely different manner than I do now.

For me, success is simple—progress toward a worthy ideal. There is no destination for success. It is only a question of growth. By adopting this mentality, it's easy to evaluate my day and ask very simply, Did I make progress toward my worthy ideal today? If so, how? And if not, why not?

Try it on!
Spend some time going into a silent space and ask yourself these questions:

- How do I define success?
- If I were successful, what would that look like, and how would it feel? How would I be living?

Be patient with the answer; let it come from deep within. The first definition on the surface is most likely one that has been programmed in by the world. If you are struggling to find an answer that resonates, try to ask the question before you fall asleep without looking for an answer. Just give it time to show up.

SETTING INTENTIONS

Once you have clearly defined what success means to you, then you can begin to set intentions for your development. These intentions will become more apparent as you develop your practice and start setting goals with an integrated approach. It is crucial to set intentions for yourself that will support your definition of success.

I like to set intentions daily within my morning and evening routines. I also set intentions for each week, month, and year. By setting an intention, you are planting a seed that will grow if you nurture it.

I've provided an example of my intentions here.

Annual Intention:

Courage

Monthly Intentions:

In my monthly intentions, I like to take an integrated approach using the three Pillars. I focus each pillar on a similar goal in life. For this example, I used the relationship with my wife. All three of my intentions are focused on deepening my relationship with her.

- **Physical:** 30 days of yoga
- **Mental:** Read The book "5 Love Languages"
- **Emotional:** Find an emotional block that keeps my marriage from evolving

Weekly Intentions:

Your weekly intention can be a quality to cultivate in your life that supports the monthly intention. A character trait that you want to strengthen. If we set the intention to enhance the quality of character throughout our week, it will be more in the front of our minds.

- Curiosity

Daily Intentions:

Setting daily intentions helps to support our weekly intentions. A small authentic action that helps support the cultivation of that quality.

- Look at my wife and see her like it's for the first time

As you set intentions, you are then able to check in with yourself and ask the questions.

Am I showing up the way I intend for myself, my family, and my community?

Again, your process of setting intentions depends on your journey and season of life. In the above example, I made the focus to be on my relationship with my wife. As we set intentions for the month, we are always approaching life from all three pillars. It helps to focus more attention on specific pillars and integrating the others as much as possible to support your growth.

SETTING MINIMUMS

Your minimums are the absolute nonnegotiable things you place in your life to support balance and growth.

By setting your daily minimums, you make sure that no matter what, you are committing to carving out a certain amount of time to focus on yourself each day, regardless of circumstances. This way, you don't get derailed by holidays, weekends, travel for work, vacations. I believe it is not only important to set daily minimums but also weekly, monthly, quarterly, and annual minimums.

I set minimums on daily practices such as my morning routine, my yoga practice, breathing exercises, reading, studying something new, etc. These minimums can change and increase as your practice evolves and your capacity expands. Revisit these minimums regularly to ensure they still work for the season of life you are in.

Setting minimums helps you stay balanced, grounded, and connected to who you are and where you are going. Let's look at some examples of minimums that you may consider.

Daily Minimums:

- 5 Minutes of Box Breathing
- 5 Minutes of Somatic Movement
- 1 Gratitude Statement
- 10 Minutes of Reading/Studying
- 5-Minute walk

Weekly Minimums:

- More extended Exercise Session 1x a Week (Run, Ruck, Hike)
- 20 Min of Box Breathing 1x a Week
- Learn Something New (Language, Guitar, New skill)

Monthly Minimums:

- Time in Nature
- Read a Book
- Connect with a Friend

Quarterly Minimums:

- Attend a New Seminar or Class
- Extended Time in Nature/Silence
- Weekend Away with Significant Other

Annual Minimums:

- Retreat with Likeminded People
- Family Vacation

Heidi and I have even gone as far as printing off an entire year's worth of calendars and designating a wall in our home office to ensure we are keeping track of and planning the minimums we have committed to. Set your minimum and watch how your life finds a flow.

FINDING MENTORSHIP

I can't stress enough the importance of mentorship. Mentors can show up in many ways. Maybe you have an old friend that you'd like to model yourself after as a father. It could be a colleague at work. If you are having a hard time finding a mentor in your life, turn to books, podcasts, etc. We should always be seeking to find the next mentor that pushes us to elevate ourselves. Find mentorship in each category. Another thing to consider is being open to hiring a coach. I have consistently worked with different coaches for years now. There is something about the commitment to growth and service when you pay someone to help guide you on your journey. The best leaders in our world have coaches. It is my opinion that every single person would benefit from coaching in all areas of life. Determine the most significant area of needed growth in your life and seek an appropriate mentor or coach.

Tip: Be cautious about following too many mentors at the same time; the message can get diluted by different approaches and opinions. Find the mentor that lights you up and makes you want to learn what they know. Or follow a mentor who is serving the world in the same capacity that you have in mind. When I first discovered Mark Divine's work with Unbeatable Mind, I immediately sought his mentorship, and continue to do so.

Connect with me personally by visiting our website at ***www.IHPcoaching.com*** where you'll find tools to provide structure and support in all of these areas.

TOOLS AND PRACTICES

Here's the part I get excited about, the tools and practices! In this section, I will define the tools and practices that are foundational to my transformation and their benefits. Then I'll give you some exercises and provide references if you want to explore further.

SOMATIC MOVEMENT

A somatic movement is when we consciously perform a movement intending to focus on the internal experience of the movement. We do this by being connected to our breath rather than the result of the movement. Yoga, Tai chi, Qi Gong are great examples. This is a practice of being and connecting with your body. Usually when we think about physical exercise we think about working our bodies to get a result. No question, having a more intense workout regimen is vital, such as cross fit, preparing for a Spartan race, etc.

It is always great to be preparing for a competition or event. I would like to offer tools to be practiced for a lifetime and done daily. The practices that improve our ability to strengthen our awareness, build our emotional intelligence, and improve spinal health. Through the practice of somatic movement, our brain and body are more connected and integrated. This can result in a reduction of chronic pain, improved digestion and sleep, and increased energy.

In my Kokoro Yoga teacher training, we were required to read many books.

One of the books was Yoga for Wellness by Gary Kraftsow. Here is a quote from the book that caught my attention and made me want to experience more of what yoga had to offer.

"At birth most of our movements are instinctive: we experience hunger or fear, and we respond by crying. As we grow, our movements gradually be-

come more and more active, more intentional, and as the mind develops, it begins in turn to program the functioning brain and body. Learning how to walk, to talk, to play, to relate with other people—acquiring these skills— we impose onto our neuromuscular structure an order that becomes pro- grammed, through repetition, into our pre-motor cortex in the form of increasingly conditioned reflexes. Where we once had to focus all our at- tention on a movement as seemingly simple as walking, we are gradually patterned to move reflexively, unconsciously. This learning process is the beginning of our conditioning, and it is why we tend, even if we don't like to admit it, to walk, talk, and behave like our parents or the people who raised us. As we continue to grow, even beyond childhood, the develop- ment of our body and mind continues to be conditioned by these twin pro- cesses of neuromuscular organization and socialization. Meanwhile, those particular patterns we each acquire and develop are always imperfect in some way, in relation to wellness: even though they allow us to function—in fact, because they allow us to function and are therefore reinforced—they inhibit our optimal development. The consequence of this conditioning is imbalance at various levels of our system, accumulation of stress, and, ul- timately, dis-ease. The good news is that things are always changing! If we can become reflectively self-conscious of our conditioned behavior, we can break the cycle by introducing new patterns of behavior that will, over time, replace the old ones and help us regain control of the direction of change in our lives. This liberation from the effects of conditioning, on all levels, is the purpose of Yoga."

Try it on!
Simply put, having a daily yoga practice is transformative. If I were to recommend one physical regimen in the journey of transformation, it would be yoga.

RESOURCES:

Gary Kraftsow, *Yoga for Wellness: Healing with the Timeless Teachings of Viniyoga*

Mark Divine, *Kokoro Yoga: Maximize Your Human Potential and Develop the Spirit*

NUTRITION AND FASTING

Note that before trying any of the nutritional approaches below, consult your healthcare professional.

Since I am by no means a nutritionist, I am going to assume that you are aware of the importance of nutrition and trust that if you need or want additional information you will find the resources that work for you.

I will, however, share the basic framework that I live by when it comes to nutrition:

- The 80/20 rule teaches you to eat with balance, moderation, and indulgence, without a guilty feeling. To be healthy and balanced, you don't always have to make 100 percent healthy food choices. Eighty percent is enough. The remaining 20 percent you can choose less healthy food and indulge yourself.
- Set minimums with fruits and vegetables every day, even if it's as simple as a bowl of carrots and broccoli with some hummus or an apple or banana.
- Drink 12–15 cups of water each day.
- Have a meal replacement shake to make life convenient and straightforward. Most days, I have one shake.
- Fast consistently. I've tried many kinds of fasting and have had different degrees of success with each. The 16/8 daily seems to be the most realistic for most people. The 16/8 is where every day you fast for 16 hours, then have an 8-hour eating window. For example, waiting until 10 am before eating anything, then making 6 pm your cutoff time for the day. I also like to incorporate a couple of 24–36 hour fasts during the month to reset my system and give my digestion a break.

Try it on!
At the end of the day, food is fuel, Figure out what works for you, and keep it simple!

BREATHWORK

Breathwork refers to any breathing exercise or technique. These techniques improve mental, physical, and emotional well-being. Focusing on the breath creates a bridge to Mental Toughness, Emotional Intelligence, and Physical Strength. During breathwork, you intentionally change your breathing pattern to influence your state of mind. Each breathing pattern has a corresponding emotional response. How do you breathe when you are panicked, frustrated, or angry compared to when you are calm, happy, and grateful? By becoming aware of your breath and taking conscious control of it, we can manage stress, guide our attention, change our state (thoughts and feelings) at will.

The average person takes between 16–20 breaths per minute, and an optimal healthy breath cadence is 6 breaths per minute. For someone who is struggling with an overactive mind or anxiety, it creates a feedback loop. Meaning, the stress causes your breath to be shallow, short, and in the chest, and your shallow breathing intensifies the anxiety. Eighty percent of people with anxiety disorders have dysfunctional breathing patterns. Breathing efficiency has been shown to be a predictor of long-term mortality in the general population. This is why I am so passionate about teaching people how to breathe correctly.

Dan Brule is a master of the breath. In his book Just Breathe, he states:

"The breathing system in most people is not functioning at an optimal level. We need to heal it. We need to improve or restore our breathing capacity, to correct any dysfunctional habits or patterns that inhibit or interfere with the free expression of our true nature and full potential. Once our breathing is full and free, healthy and natural, once it is restored or raised to an optimal level, then it automatically becomes a therapeutic tool. The body and breath can be used to heal the mind, and the mind and breath can be used to heal the body. Breathwork can be used to heal attitudes, emotions, and behaviors."

Not only does proper breathing help with anxiety and depression, it acts as a healing tool. It can also improve our overall performance in life and as an athlete.

Patrick Mckeown is also one of my mentors in breathwork. I am a certified instructor through his Oxygen Advantage program. In his book The Oxygen Advantage, his focus is on performance. He states: "If we breathe better, increasing the amount of carbon dioxide inside us, then we can deliver more oxygen to our muscles and organs, including the heart and brain, and thus heighten our physical capacity."

Basic Tips for Getting Started with Breathing Techniques:

- Sit up straight, with a slight tuck of your chin, close your eyes or soft glaze
- Nostril breathing
- Breathe light and slow
- Breathe deep into lower ribs using the diaphragm
- Keep your attention on your breath—when your mind wanders, bring it back to your breath

Breath Assessment:

If you answer yes to any of these questions, you may have a breathing pattern disorder.

- Wake up with a dry mouth?
- Sigh or yawn frequently?
- Cold hands and feet?
- Tense throughout the day?

Other Signs of Improper Breath Patterns:

- Lower back pain
- Breathe through mouth
- Breathlessness at rest
- Poor concentration
- Feeling anxious
- Irritability
- Wake up in the middle of the night
- Snoring
- Insomnia

Of all the areas I've studied, I've found that breathwork has been the one that has the most conflicting opinions and approaches. There are a ton of people practicing breathwork and selling programs that are not focusing on the science and mechanics of it. I've gone to great lengths to ensure I fully understand what is happening, so that I'm sure that what I'm practicing will produce the long-term effect I seek. I urge you to find again someone that is experienced and understands the breath to be a mentor.

Try it on!
Regular Breathing or Tactical Breathing Coaching Points:

- Focus on breathing
- Breathe smooth, deep, light, and quiet
- 5 second Inhale – 5 second Exhale
- Learn to flow back and forth between passive and active breathing, or between breath Awareness and Conscious breathing

---

RESOURCES:

Dan Brule, *Just Breathe: Mastering Breathwork for Success in Life, Love, Business, and Beyond*

Patrick Mckeown, *The Oxygen Advantage: Simple, Scientifically Proven Breathing Techniques to Help You Become Healthier, Slimmer, Faster, and Fitter*

VISUALIZATION

Visualization is a powerful tool that can be split into two categories, Mental Projection and Mental Rehearsal.

- Mental Projection is when you see yourself from the wish-fulfilled or end state where you've already achieved the goal.
- Mental Rehearsal is simply to practice the task or skill in your mind's eye. This is done in the first person or third person. To see yourself being successful, healthy, grounded. To have experience as your future self. By practicing this daily, we are priming our body and brain—we are setting up the neurological hardware to make it easier to achieve our desired state or experience. Your body doesn't know the difference between imagination and reality. Therefore, as you rehearse and imagine yourself in future states, you begin to draw those experiences into the present moment and experience more of them. This is a skill and can be developed like anything else. Be patient and practice, and over time you will see incredible results that will change your life.

I want to give you one example of how visualization has been such a powerful tool for me. A few years ago when I first started studying Unbeatable Mind, I was into training with bodyweight exercises. I would set a goal to perform a skill, such as a muscle-up. One of my goals was to do 10 handstand pushups (supported by the wall). For someone who used to be overweight and has shoulder issues from playing college football, this was a considerable challenge. I trained for months, using the wall to support myself. I created a progression on how to prepare to strengthen the muscles that I would need to perform this skill. I probably trained for five to six months and was making hardly any improvement. I still couldn't even do one rep, much less reach my goal of 10. Frustration set in and I was on the verge of giving up. I realized my mind wasn't on board with this specific goal. I would begin to attempt a handstand pushup, and there was this tiny voice saying, Don't hurt your shoulder. You can't do it.

I decided to take this goal from the physical outward actions to the process of visualization. I stopped all physical training for six weeks and trained mentally instead. I spent time every day seeing myself doing the handstand pushups, rehearsing every step and generating the feeling behind completing them. I rehearsed it in the first person, seeing myself complete every rep with perfect form and a full range of motion. Three weeks in, I felt the urge to try and see if this process was working. I went out to my garage gym, and without any hesitation or doubt I pumped out six reps. Three weeks later, I told Heidi that I was going to attempt my 10-rep challenge. I knew the extra motivation of having someone watching would give the little extra boost I needed. I got warmed up and powered through all 10 reps of handstand push-ups like it was nothing. It solidified the power of the mind. I trained by winning in my mind first, giving my body the experience of achieving the goal. I was strong enough to accomplish it all along. I just had to see it in my mind.

RESOURCES:

Mark Divine with Allyson E. Machate, The Way of the SEAL: Think Like an Elite Warrior to Lead and Succeed

MEDITATION

We cannot always rely on our external circumstances as the source of our satisfaction. Meditation, however, can deliver something much more significant—happiness independent of conditions.
– Shinzen Young

There are numerous types of meditation. Some focus on building concentration or attention control; some are aimed toward insight or exploring the nature of consciousness.

The first principle of meditation is increasing concentration. Concentration is just like a muscle; it can be trained and strengthened. The degree of strengthening will depend on how consistent you are and for how long. When you develop concentration in your morning routine, it will be available to you all day, improving your performance in all areas of life. There isn't any aspect of life that is not enhanced by our ability to be present and focused. After practicing meditation for years now, I've found levels of concentration that I never knew were possible. For example, I used to read a paragraph, then had no idea what I just read. But just last night while the kids were practicing karate in the living room and Heidi was doing dishes while listening to music, I was able to read with no problem at all. This would have been impossible for me just a few years ago.

Meditation also makes it possible to build your awareness. A meditative practice becomes impactful when you find yourself in a meditative state throughout the day. You naturally find yourself there when driving a car, washing the dishes, or having a conversation with a family member or friend.

So, what is mediation good for? In my opinion, it is useful for everything! The benefits of meditation are endless. I listed a few that may resonate with you. Too many benefits to list them all here.

Benefits of Meditation include:

- Improved Concentration
- Enhanced Self Awareness
- Reduced Stress
- Increased Immunity
- Decrease Blood Pressure
- Helps Control Anxiety
- Promotes Emotional Health
- Makes Positive Behavior Changes
- Live More Authentically
- Helps Control Pain
- Improves Sleep, Sex, and Energy
- Reduces Memory Loss
- Provides Sense of Calm, Peace, and Balance
- More Connected to Nature

Try it on!
Beginning Meditative Progression:

1. Sit erect, let your thoughts roam where they will, but be perfectly still for five minutes to continue this until you have control over your physical body.

2. Focus on breath, taking in only the air that you need and breathe with such lightness that you do not disturb the hairs in your nose.

3. Relax, let go, remove all pressure from the nerves. Relaxation is an absolute necessity to allow the mind to quiet. Mentally determine that you will relax every muscle and nerve until you feel quiet and restful and at peace with yourself and the world.

4. Focus on only your breath. Every time your mind wanders, gently come back to your breath. The goal is to shorten the amount of time between when you lose your focus on your breathing and you come back to it.

5. Focus on Nostrils as you breathe while witnessing thoughts, feelings, and sounds—labeling "thought, feeling, hearing" as you become aware of them coming up and pull your awareness back to your breath with no judgment.

6. Sit perfectly still, drop all labeling and all thought. Continue to return to no thought every time you wander, seek silence by just being, let go completely, and just become the silence.

7. Mentally create or select a sacred place. Make a complete mental picture of it—see the grounds, the trees, everything.

RESOURCES:

Shinzen Young, The Science of Enlightenment: How Meditation Works

JOURNALING

Journaling is an easy and accessible tool. It allows for insights, inspiration, and creativity. Writing down thoughts, fears, judgments, etc., will allow you to look at your thoughts and separate from them to let them go. We can notice patterns that may require attention and healing.

It is also beneficial to journal in order to keep track of your progress as you evolve. It is easy to lose track of how far we have come. It is always powerful to go back and read journal entries from a year or two ago and be reminded how far you've come.

Try it on!
Free write 5–10 minutes in your morning routine or evening routine. Just sit down with a journal in hand and begin writing. Don't let the pen stop no matter what comes out, don't judge or analyze it, just let it flow. This has been my primary journaling exercise over the years and has allowed me to capture the thoughts and ideas that turned into this book and our coaching program. Another great way to journal is to have a structured daily planner that has a list of questions and intentions to keep you on track. Here is the link to the daily planner that we use in our coaching membership.

Download our Printable Daily Planner at www.ihpcoaching.com

MORNING ROUTINES

"We are what we repeatedly do. Excellence, then, is not an act, but a habit." - Aristotle

Having a morning routine is the foundational discipline that initiates the right mindset and leads to all other practice throughout the day. Morning routines change regularly, depending on what season of life you are in. I will share how I start my day so that you can have an idea of what it could look like.

One of the first and most important aspects of having a morning routine is to have a designated space for your practice. Also, make sure the night before you have set yourself up for success. For example, I have a glass of water next to my bed so that when I wake up, the very first thing I do is drink it.

Getting Started:

- Designate an area or space for your morning routine and prepare it for practice
- Plan your morning routine; write it out in detail
- Set a minimum time and practice
- Have other materials ready: journal, book, headphones, etc.

My Morning Routine:

As I awake, I begin by becoming aware of my breath and taking my first intentional breath of the day with a sense of gratitude. I then become aware of my first thought and make sure it is one of positivity and is serving my highest good. I then put my feet flat on the floor and have that full glass of water that I placed next to my bed. Once I have done my morning business, it is downstairs to my place of practice, and I do some somatic movement for about 10 minutes while listening to a recording of my mission statement and cultivating a stronger sense of gratitude. Then I go into my breathwork, which varies depending on what my intention is for my practice. Usually, it will include some form of box breathing, then I go into my Unbeatable Mind continuum practice of Attention control, Witnessing, then Insight meditation. Following insight meditation, I go through quick visualization of my future self, current mission in life and then-current day mission, making sure I am clear about what my focus is for the day. I then end with a practice called sacred first word. This is a practice in the warrior tradition, used after a period of silence where you speak out loud your intention. For example, I would say a single word, such as "courageous." It is spoken quietly so only you can hear it. Then I go into either journaling, writing, or studying time where I like to fill my head with new information before I do my longer yoga session or a workout.

- First Breath and First Thought
- Water
- Somatic Movement + Access a Feeling of Gratitude
- Breathwork + Meditation + Visualization

- Sacred First Word
- Journaling + Study Something New + Write
- Yoga or Workout

If I do the entire morning routine, it takes two hours. I understand this may seem like a lot if you are just getting started. Not every day is this extensive, but I do have my minimum practice that takes 20 minutes. Years ago, when I first started doing my morning routine, it was straightforward and short. It has evolved and changed over the years and will evolve as I continue to grow.

The point is to start the day with consistency and with intention. By setting up a morning routine that supports your practices, you are making a statement to yourself and the Universe, saying this is who I've come here to be. It is incredibly powerful and carries you through the day.

MORNING ROUTINE EXAMPLES

- ❏ Drink Water or Tea
- ❏ Breath Practice
- ❏ Heart Coherence
- ❏ Set a Daily Intention
- ❏ Grounding or Earthing
- ❏ Cold Exposure (Cold Shower)
- ❏ Meditation
- ❏ Visualization
- ❏ Prayer
- ❏ Read or Study
- ❏ Journal or Free Writing

- ❏ Gratitude Statements
- ❏ Mirror Work
- ❏ Recite Positive Affirmations
- ❏ Yoga or Mindful Movement
- ❏ Review Daily Tasks
- ❏ Time Block Schedule
- ❏ Review Long Term Goals
- ❏ Review Personal Ethos
- ❏ Make Your Bed
- ❏ Eat a healthy Breakfast
- ❏ Vitamins/Supplements

Try it on!
Build Your Own: Morning Routine

Set your minimum of how you will start each day. Keep it simple to start. Be clear about your intention for each morning routine to help you build this powerful practice of beginning each day with a purpose.

Eight Week Morning Routine Progression:

WEEKS 1-2

Week 1 (5 Min)

Wake-up Time _____

Water
1 Min Gratitude Practice
2 Min Somatic Movement
1 Min Breath Awareness
1 Min Set Intention for the day

Week 2 (8 Min)

Wake-up Time _____

Water
1 Min Gratitude Practice
2 Min Somatic Movement
2 Min Breath Awareness
2 Min Conscious Slow, Light, Deep Breathing
1 Min Set Intention for the day

WEEKS 3-4

Week 3 (10 Min)

Wake-up Time _____

Water
1 Min Gratitude Practice
2 Min Somatic Movement
3 Min Breath Awareness
3 Min Conscious Slow, Light, Deep Breathing
1 Min Set Intention for the day

Week 4 (12 Min)

Wake-up Time _____

Water
1 Min Gratitude Practice
2 Min Somatic Movement
4 Min Breath Awareness
4 Min Conscious Slow, Light, Deep Breathing
1 Min Set Intention for the day

WEEKS 5-6

Week 5 (15 Min)

Wake-up Time _____

Water
1 Min Gratitude Practice
3 Min Somatic Movement
5 Min Breath Awareness
5 Min Conscious Slow, Light, Deep Breathing
1 Min Set Intention for the day

Week 6 (18 Min)

Wake-up Time _____

Water
1 Min Gratitude Practice
5 Min Somatic Movement
5 Min Breath Awareness
5 Min Conscious Slow, Light, Deep Breathing
1 Min Visualize Ideal Self/Vision
1 Min Set Intention for the day

WEEKS 7-8

Week 7 (20 Min)

Wake-up Time _____

Water
1 Min Gratitude Practice
5 Min Somatic Movement
5 Min Breath Awareness
5 Min Conscious Slow, Light, Deep Breathing
3 Min Visualize Ideal Self/Vision
1 Min Set Intention for the day

Week 8 (25 Min)

Wake-up Time _____

Water
1 Min Gratitude Practice
5 Min Somatic Movement
5 Min Breath Awareness
5 Min Conscious Slow, Light, Deep Breathing
3 Min Witnessing/Labeling Thoughts and Feelings
5 Min Visualize Ideal Self/Vision
1 Min Set Intention for the day

EVENING ROUTINE AND SLEEP HYGIENE

Practicing healthy sleep habits is vital for both physical and mental health. It can also improve productivity and overall quality of life. Everyone, from children to older adults, can benefit from practicing good sleep habits. We spend up to one-third of our lives asleep. Operating from sleep deprivation was normal for me for many years. I had forgotten what being truly rested felt like. When I started making sleep a priority was when I found it made all other aspects of the day that much easier. When you look at the effect of sleep on our mental and physical performance, it takes on a whole new meaning.

Benefits of getting quality sleep:

- Improves Concentration, Productivity, Cognition
- Helps us Manage Stress
- Lowered Risk of Weight Gain
- Improved Physical Performance
- Decreased Risk of Depression
- Lower Inflammation
- Improves Emotional Intelligence
- Improves Memory
- Boosts Immunity

Tips for good sleep hygiene:

- Avoid looking at screens two hours before bedtime (including cell phone)
- Have your last meal two hours before bedtime
- Keep the room temperature around 67 degrees
- Black out room using room darkening curtains
- Sleep with your mouth closed (tape mouth shut using special mouth tapes if necessary)

Your evening routine can be just as impactful as a morning routine. I like to keep my evening routine as simple as possible. I use our Daily Planner to keep myself on track.

Here's my 3-step evening process:

1. Reflect to learn from the day, then let it go.
2. Prepare for the morning routine.
3. Cultivate emotional connection to my future self.

Try it on!
Create your evening routine using the tips above.

SPOT DRILLS

Spot drills are a tool that comes from our Unbeatable Mind training. They are used throughout the day to regain connection and focus on our intention. I like to use spot drills when I notice myself dropping into negative thinking and I want to transmute negative thought into positive emotions. I also use check-ins with myself to keep on track. It is easy to lose track of the cumulative stressors as we navigate the day.

We use spot drills to eradicate that build-up and give us a fresh start as many times as needed. I have reminders set on my phone four times a day to do a check-in and see if a spot drill may be required. If so, I stop what I am doing and practice a quick five min drill.

Benefits of doing regular spot drills:

- Arousal control
- Combat compound effect of stress throughout the day
- Check-in with intention
- Shift state if necessary
- Bring conscious awareness to the present moment

Daily Check-In Questions:

- Who am I being?
- What do I need to do to reconnect or stay connected?

Spot drills can be breathing and movement practices, and more. Spot drills become that much more powerful when you layer them together—for example, doing power posing, standing in a mountain pose, and taking intentional breaths while visualizing your future self. Five minutes can be incredibly impactful to your day.

Here are some examples:

- 5 Minutes of Conscious Breathing
- 50 Air Squats
- 10 Sun Salutations
- 30 Burpees
- Brisk Walk Around the Block
- Power Posing (Posturing)
- Resourcing
- Grounding
- Cold Exposure
- Positive Music

Try it on!

Try Grounding: Either in a seated position or standing, feel your hands and feet. Describe what is happening in them. Notice your hands; put your attention on the space between your first two fingers. As you move your attention to the peripheral parts of the nervous system, it gives the central core some relief. Feel your back against the chair, then turn your attention to the breath.

Try Resourcing: (going to your happy place): Take a moment to imagine being in a familiar place or a place in your imagination where you are most settled and calm. This is called the "Mind Gym" in Unbeatable Mind. It is a place to train and visualize winning in your mind.

RESOURCES:

Mark Divine with Allyson E. Machate, *The Way of the SEAL: Think Like an Elite Warrior to Lead and Succeed*

Mark Divine, *Unbeatable Mind: Forge Resiliency and Mental Toughness to Succeed at an Elite Level*

GOING DEEPER

In this section, I will share some of the most transformative tools I've used for going deeper into my growth and healing.

SHADOW WORK

When it comes to individual growth that makes a significant impact on our inner world and how we experience life, as well as on our environment, there is no more important work we can do than shadow work.

Shadow work is learning how to access certain agreements or beliefs, formed in our childhood, that shape the way we view the world and therefore limit us. As we are more able to access those limiting beliefs about ourselves and our circumstances, we can find the cause in our actions and thoughts. When we understand where things originate, we can rewrite the narrative to serve the outcomes we desire in life. Learning how to access our emotions without labeling them as good or bad but understanding that they are just what we are experiencing will open us up to more empathy, compassion, resiliency, forgiveness, and acceptance. We will become more authentic. An example of a shadow at work in our life is when we want the approval of others, or we care what they think. This comes from a part of our psyche that we can access through doing shadow work. There are multiple types of shadow work. The Q Process has been the most impactful to my own journey, truly providing a tool that can be developed and integrated into everyday life. Heidi and I are both Certified Q Process Facilitators. Here is some basic information on the Q Process from the website. When you are ready, we will be here to support you in this important transformational work.

About The Q Process™

The Mindfulness Center in Southern Maine identifies the five core skills of mindfulness as:

Clarifying, setting, and reaffirming intention: What am I practicing?

Cultivating a witnessing awareness: Developing meta-cognition, state awareness, and practicing outer non-reactivity while witnessing the inner landscape.

Stabilizing Attention: Staying focused, placing attention on your intention.

Strengthening Self-Regulation: Settling negative energy intentionally, bringing the whole brain back online.

Practicing Loving Kindness: Calming the inner critic and self-judgment, practicing non-judgmental awareness and kindness and compassion for yourself and others.

The Q Process integrates these five principles in a 21-day structured reflection tool to reframe triggering experiences. The 21 days are made up of three seven-day phases.

Phase One focuses on critical thoughts or discordant behaviors that may have been directed outwardly. Phase Two focuses on any critical thoughts the participant has directed inwardly (self-criticism, self-judgment) that trigger shame, anxiety, etc., from old firing patterns.

Phase Three follows both internal and external triggers into the past to find a memory associated with the pattern and uses a meditative visualization to loosen its emotional associations, allowing the neural firing pattern to shift.

As people become more practiced with the worksheets, they can gain incredible insights into their core self and their core wounds. They are able to separate their new, emerging sense of self (as defined by way of being) from the habitual "selves" that have their roots in unmet childhood needs and have often been strengthened and made more rigid in adulthood. Old patterns are revealed, and a new way of seeing the self emerges.

Some participants report immediate success in differentiating themselves from their patterns, and this brings some relief. They see they have a pattern, but they are not the pattern. While it is not the objective of the 21 days to bring about a cessation of all habitual behavior, it is intended to offer participants an opportunity to develop a new habit of "seeing," one in which they develop a witnessing presence, where they come to observe themselves, even in real time.

RESOURCE:

The Q Process™ www.theqeffect.com

Here is a real-life example of how I used The Q Process to transform a limiting belief and heal myself:

Early on in running my business, I took on a commercial painting project outside my area of expertise. I had already completed the job when the company told me that I did not meet vendor requirements, meaning they would not pay me until I finished the required vendor packet. As I read through the requirements, I realized that there was a ton of info I didn't know or had not completed—for example, a 30-hour OSHA class on safety, hazard plans for employees, etc.

As I was processing this information, I identified the feelings and thoughts that were touched by this situation as overwhelmed, anxious, and embarrassed.

Rather than ignore these feelings as I'd done in the past, and shrinking my comfort zone by doing so, I used the practice to help stay connected to the discomfort and be curious about what it was that was genuinely causing these feelings. The Q process strengthens my awareness of these uncomfortable feelings and thoughts and helps me uncover what is underneath it.

As I sat with these feelings from a non-judgmental and curious view, I was taken back to the fourth grade, to the moment when my parents learned I was reading at only first grade level. I should probably mention that my parents were both educators—Dad was a high school principal and my mom was a teacher at my elementary school. I remember my Dad sitting me on the bed and asking me to read to him. I remember he asked my mom, "How did this happen?" The more frustrated he got, the harder it was to read. Looking back on this, I realized that as a result I had taken on a limiting belief about myself: I am stupid. I am a disappointment. Back in the present, I was able to find compassion for 10-year-old Ryan.

I was so grateful to uncover this pattern so I could begin to heal and change this belief. This belief does not serve me and never has. I could describe countless times where I held back or hid from the world to try and protect myself so people wouldn't find out that I was stupid. So many times in my life, in school or work, the moment that something challenged my intellect I would just shut down or escape.

Understanding that there are so many ways that this experience could have gone, I went into a heart-centered place. I released this belief that I received back into all possibilities with complete compassion for everybody involved, knowing that we were all doing our best. I felt a massive release in my chest and felt lighter as this story was released, like a heavy weight had been lifted from my shoulders.

Next, I began the process of repairing my childhood self by choosing a new, more loving and helpful experience and message. Here is how I reimagined that moment.

My parents realized I was struggling to read. My dad sat me down with complete patience and compassion. He had everyone leave the room so we could communicate without judgment from others. He reassured me, saying, "Ryan, you are safe with me; we're in this together. Will you do your best to read this for me?" As I struggled to read, he praised me for my effort. He taught me how as we grow and overcome obstacles in life, we become stronger. "Ryan, this is one of the many obstacles that you will face in life; the obstacle itself does not define you. It is your attitude and effort as you face the obstacle head-on that defines you. We'll work through this together, and you'll be stronger because of it." Again, he assured me, "Ryan, you are smart and safe, and we're in this together!"

As a result, the new message I received about myself was that I am smart, safe, and I can overcome any obstacle.

I could easily imagine many ways life would have been different growing up with that new belief. I adopted a growth mindset from that moment forward. I began to enjoy school just for the challenge of it. I enjoyed learning new things and found myself welcoming challenges and enjoyed stepping outside of my comfort zone.

Now turning back to the present-day trigger, I could see that being with my Q Qualities Confident and Poised could have helped me respond in a better way and not feel diminished. I imagined a RE-DO, and I could see how different it felt!

My redo looked something like this, As I read the requirements for the Vendor Packet, I stayed open and welcomed the challenge. I am confident and poised to know that there isn't anything I cannot do if I face the obstacle head-on. I am excited to see what new possibilities and growth can come from this situation.

To make this new way of being an integrated part of who I am today, I took the authentic action to call the accountant for the company and ask for help, as well as communicate my lack of knowledge in the situation. This helped me restore balance and anchor in me a sense of confidence and poise and meet my need for safety and security. A lesson I have learned that can be hard as a man is to ask for help. I have found since doing this work that I am so much more aware of this trigger and catch it very quickly. I am able to relate to my Q qualities and take the authentic action in the moment to maintain balance in my life and continue to reinforce this new message and belief. This new belief is becoming the predominant thought and feeling, moreso each day.

AUTOSUGGESTION

Autosuggestion Is the process of influencing your subconscious mind by suggesting to it who you are through spoken words and imagery that cultivate an elevated emotional response. Dull and unemotional terms will not be accepted as truth. To get the subconscious mind to take the suggestion, you will need to feel it.

There are many ways to do this work. The common methods of gratitude practice, affirmations, or mantras are all excellent tools. But, if you are willing to do some extra work and go deeper into the creative process to use your imagination and create a clear image and feeling of your future self and future experiences, you can accelerate the process of influencing your subconscious mind.

The next three exercises—who am I being, personal mission statement, and vision cards, will help you create the content that you can use to suggest to yourself.

WHO AM I BEING?

This is an exercise that helps us create the content for scripting, which we'll get to later. How often as a father/mother, husband/wife, son/daughter, neighbor, or friend, do we feel we could have done better, or we didn't show up as our true selves? How often are we left with a sense of regret or guilt because we missed an opportunity to experience what fills us up the most?

Do you fear you will look back and have a list of could haves, would haves, and should haves?

Living from could haves, would haves, and should haves is just reliving the past and creating the future at the same time. Your body doesn't know the difference between an actual event or you remembering it. Therefore, as we replay that event in our minds, we feel guilt, shame, regret. We are reinforcing it through the same neurological pathway, and it is more likely to happen again. We should use the negative emotions and experiences as teaching tools, be grateful for the knowledge, then turn them into wisdom by replacing it with what better serves us.

We can turn every experience, emotion, feeling, and thought into a learning experience. In our day to day life, we focus so much on doing. We measure our success and happiness based on how much we got done. It was a good day because I... or it was a bad day because I didn't. Rather than focusing on our doing and the external environment, we need to look at the internal environment and focus our energy and attention on who it is we are being.

Another way of putting it is by focusing on how we are showing up for ourselves and others. Who are we being with what we are having and who are we being with what we are doing? What is our state?

In this exercise, we will equip ourselves with the proper tools to construct the version of ourself that makes conscious decisions from our true essence and reminds us who we have come here to be.

Self-realization is a practice. To practice, we must go into our mind and use it as a workshop to create our future self. Let's go into our workshop!

Step one: Make a list of six individuals: personal heroes or people you admire. They could be living or dead, historical or fictional. Each must possess qualities that you value or attributes you wish for yourself.

Step two: Beside each person, briefly list the qualities you admire in them. The quality reflects why this person is on your list. For example, if one of your heroes is Superman, beside his name you might list strong, courageous, service-oriented, etc. Use one word or two-word terms to identify the attribute or quality. (Reference qualities sheet for additional ideas.)

Step Three: Circle the eight qualities that resonate with you the most.

Step Four: Next, determine the roles you play in your daily life. You will notice that the first category is created for you.

Example: Who am I being as ... in relationship to myself. The others could be father/mother, husband/wife, son/daughter, friend, mentor, employee, employer, or whatever roles you play in your own life.

Step Five: We now need to list three ways that we want to show up as each of these roles, using the list you created and referencing the Example Qualities list for additional ideas.

Remember, this is a projection of your future or ideal self. Make sure not to limit yourself in any way. This is a chance to use your God-given gift of imagination!

People **Qualities**

1. _____ _____ _____ _____

2. _____ _____ _____ _____

3. _____ _____ _____ _____

4. _____ _____ _____ _____

5. _____ _____ _____ _____

6. _____ _____ _____ _____

EXAMPLE QUALITIES

Aware	Courageous	Organized	Peaceful
Trustworthy	Present	Passionate	Flexible
Accepting	Honest	Inventive	Spontaneous
Optimistic	Creative	Adventurous	Nonjudgemental
Spiritual	Helpful	Funny	Consistent
Kind	Empathetic	Energetic	Harmonious
Ambitious	Patient	Committed	Goofy
Thorough	Balanced	Fulfilled	Thoughtful
Intelligent	Determined	Healthy	Friendly
Intuitive	Purposeful	Nurturing	Confident
Caring	Sociable	Outgoing	Motivated
Open Minded	Charming	Willing	Serious
Assertive	Loving	Positive	Independent
Loyal	Decisive	Sensitive	Trustung
Inspiring	Responsible	Enthusiastic	Resilient
Authentic	Grounded	Focused	Disciplined
Available	Humble	Welcoming	Relatable
Respectful	Transparent	Generous	

Who am I being as ... in relationship to myself.	
Qualities	Feelings

Experience Statement:

Who am I being as...	
Qualities	Feelings

Experience Statement:

Who am I being as...	
Qualities	Feelings

Experience Statement:

Who am I being as...	
Qualities	Feelings

Experience Statement:

EXAMPLE FEELINGS

Affectionate
Compassioante
Friendly
Loving
Open-Hearted
Empathetic
Tender
Warm

Confident
Empowered
Open
Proud
Safe
Secure

Joyful
Delighted
Glad
Happy
Pleased
Tickled

Engaged
Alert
Curious
Engrossed
Enchanted
Entranced
Fascinated
Interested
Intrigued
Involved

Exhilarated
Blissful
Ecstatic
Elated
Enthralled
Exuberant
Radiant
Thrilled

Refreshed
Revived
Rejuvenated
Renewed
Rested
Restored

Excited
Amazed
Aroused
Astonished
Dazzled
Eager
Energetic
Enthusiastic
Giddy
Invigorated

Grateful
Appreciative
Moved
Thankful
Touched

Hopeful
Expectant
Encouraged

Inspired
Amazed
Awed

Peaceful
Calm
Clear Headed
Comfortable
Centered
Content
Fulfilled
Mellow
Quiet
Relaxed
Relieved
Satisfied
Serene
Still
Tranquil
Trusting

Step Six: Now, reference the feeling chart and describe each quality with a feeling or two that you will experience by showing up as your ideal self. Think of the impact you will be having on others and your environment because of being this version of you. How does that make you feel?

Step Seven: Write an experience statement for each role you play in life using the qualities you came up with for each, incorporating the feelings.

Experience Statement: Stated in the first or second person, present tense, describes your qualities and feelings in detail, positively stated, filter out any never, don't, or other resistant words.

Example in Second Person:

You are so patient and gracious with your wife every day. You are supportive, loving, and compassionate with her. You are such a fantastic listener and always give her room to grow. We are comfortable communicating with a calm and open heart.

PERSONAL MISSION STATEMENT

A personal mission statement defines who you are and what you stand for as a person. It clearly states your purpose and principles in life. It defines how you will live out those principles and purposes through family and occupation. It should be clear to you after writing a personal mission statement what matters the most to you. It is not a stagnant piece of work that you write once then etch into stone. It is something you work on, then set aside and revisit every few months to rewrite and gain more clarity as you grow. Take your time to answer these questions.

Getting started:

- What does success look like for you?
- What or who is most important to you?
- What are your grounding principles?
- What impact would you like to make within your family and community?
- Who are you being, or how do you want to act?
- How do you want to treat people?

Example answers:

Success is progress toward a worthy ideal

- My family, friends, and colleagues
- Lead with love, focus on growth and curiosity
- Balance work and family, loyalty, trust
- Leadership
- Open, compassionate, patient, loving

Personal Mission Statement Example:

My Definite purpose in life is to learn continually, grow, and give. I am on a mission to become the highest expression of myself so my children learn what is truly possible through love and faith. I use my energy and inspiration to build relationships that promote growth for all in an unconditionally loving way, leaning into resistance with patience and compassion for myself and others. I am loyal, honest, and transparent with friends and family. Every time I look at my family, I am reminded why I do the work and to keep going!

VISION CARDS

Vision cards are an exercise using 3x5 notecards to help create an emotional connection to vision. I like this simple exercise to use our imagination and create some clarity around what our future may look and feel like. The objective is to be just specific enough to be able to have an emotional charge but not to be so detailed that we limit ourselves with our conscious mind. We want to leave room for the subconscious mind to use interpretation. You are just planting the seed of intention, then allowing for things to show up.

This is an exercise that is best done right before going to sleep as a potential part of your evening routine.

How it works:

Front of Card (Doing):

- Write down your goal
- Activities associated with the goal
- Titles and description of the goal

Back of Card (Being):

- Impact this achievement is making on you, your family and community or business
- Emotions associated with making this impact (how does it make you feel)
- What qualities were shown to achieve this goal?

Tips:

- Feel free to use drawings, stars. Circle words or phrases, underline words. The more energy you put into each card, the better.
- Do as many cards as you wish.
- Put them somewhere safe and forget about them. Remember, you are planting the seed of intention, then letting it go.
- Revisit every few months to see what has changed, what may need to be recharged.

Vision Card Examples:

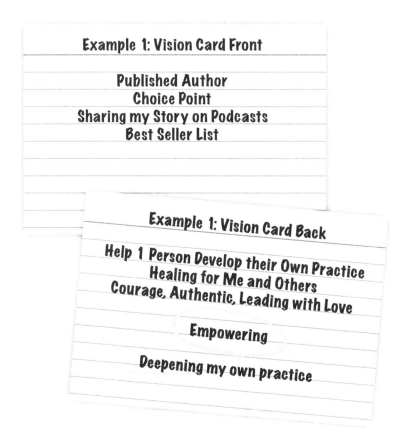

Example 1: Vision Card Front

Published Author
Choice Point
Sharing my Story on Podcasts
Best Seller List

Example 1: Vision Card Back

Help 1 Person Develop their Own Practice
Healing for Me and Others
Courage, Authentic, Leading with Love

Empowering

Deepening my own practice

Try it on!
Create your own vision cards for each area of your life or specific goal.

SCRIPTING

I have come up with a process for autosuggestion that I call scripting. I use a combination of the content from who am I being, personal mission statement, and vision cards to write out a script. Then I record it in my own voice to relaxing or meditative music. I listen to these recordings just before I fall asleep. Most nights I fall asleep while listening. I've been using this practice for years now and am always amazed at the influence it has on my subconscious mind. I find myself living out the qualities and activities from the scripts, and realize after the fact—oh yeah, that was in my script.

Just before you fall asleep is the most critical moment in transformation. As we are falling asleep and our conscious mind begins to relax and detach, our subconscious mind becomes open to suggestion. The final state (thoughts, feelings) is what the subconscious mind will accept. Our subconscious mind is also very suggestable first thing in the morning and after a hard workout or long period of silence. This is the best time to practice autosuggestion.

You can use these scripts to suggest to your subconscious mind who you will wake up as tomorrow. Start with simple suggestions like, "When you awake, you will be calm, focused, and connected to your breath. You will start your day with intention."

Notice, I use the second person. There is a new science in sports psychology showing that self-talk in the second person is more effective than first person. For example, "You can do this" will help you perform better in a difficult situation than "I can do this." This science is new and suggests that it creates self-distancing, which makes it more like you are coaching yourself. It encourages more of an observer role. My experience is that I feel more accessible and perform better when I speak to myself in the second person. I encourage you to try writing your scripts in both first and second person to see what feels more authentic and empowering to you. Everybody will have a different experience.

Tip: Listen to the script consistently for 21 days and then set it down for a week to recognize the programming that you created. For example, if you listen to a morning script every day for 21 days, on the 22nd day when you set it down you will notice the automatic loops that are consistent with your script. If you have in your script to find one thing to be grateful for, you may notice that you automatically ask yourself, "What am I grateful for?"

Writing Your Evening Script:

- Induction
- Breathing techniques to aid in preparing my mind and body for sleep
- Questioning
- Complete the Day: Process the day, then visualize yourself cutting the cord from the day to let it go
- Who Are You Being?
- Use your Vision Cards to Create Statements from a place of already having achieved or possessing the quality or goal
- Closing

EVENING SCRIPT EXAMPLE:

Take a deep breath... (Induction/ Breath Awareness)

Evening Breath Ratio (4-2-8) 4 second inhale, 2-second hold, 8-second exhale.

How did I do today? (Questioning)

What would I have done differently?

What did I learn?

What did I do well?

Now let go of the day, deep breath in and out, let it go, visualize cutting the cord. (Complete the Day)

You continue to live with the mentality always to learn, grow, and give. You are grateful for the abundant health and happiness in your life. You are mentally strong, confident, humble, while still being fierce! You live courageously and always lean into resistance with love and compassion for yourself and others. You are extremely consistent with your daily practices to stay connected to God and his divine power. Your patience is unmatched. You find joy in every moment.

You are healthy and in excellent physical shape. You are continually training your body to become a tool for success. You are entirely aware of your breath. You do daily breathing exercises and incorporate spot drills multiple times every day. You are flexible, strong, and have high endurance. You have made Kokoro yoga a daily practice and love how it makes you feel. Every single day you are stronger than the day before. You continue to unlock your full potential by fully integrating your whole self.

You are patient and gracious with your wife every day. You are supportive, loving, and compassionate with her. You are such a fantastic listener and always give her room to grow. We are comfortable communicating with a calm and open heart.

You are blessed with creativity and ideas that you use to empower yourself and thousands of others. You have written your book about your transformation. It is a fantastic catalyst for your coaching business and speaking career. It has made the best-seller list. You are on one podcast after another sharing your story. By sharing this and writing this book, you are impacting thousands of people. (Who are You Being?)

A higher concept of yourself is waiting for you when you awake. (Closing)

Writing Your Morning Script:

- Induction
- Breath Awareness: Connect to your breath
- Grounding: Become aware of your feet contacting the floor
- Gratitude: Find something to be grateful for and give yourself time to feel it while maintaining a healthy breathing pattern (5-second Inhale, 5-second exhale)
- Mission Statement, Personal Ethos, and Definite Purpose
- Vision Questions
  - 25 Year
  - Current Mission
  - Today's Mission
- Powerful Question and Mantra

MORNING SCRIPT EXAMPLE:

Take an intentional breath... (Induction/ Breath Awareness)

Feel your feet on the ground... (Grounding)

What are you grateful for? (Gratitude)

Bring this image to your heart space while breathing deeply...

Let this feeling spread through your entire body...

Your Definite purpose in life is to have everlasting persistence in self-mastery. You are on a mission to become the highest expression of yourself, so your children learn what is truly possible through love and faith. You are always connected to your true self and live with obedience to universal laws, which gives you uncommon resolve. Your unwavering faith in the laws gives you the courage to continue to venture into the unknown to create and develop a lifestyle that empowers yourself and others, gives us permission to feel, and to be free. You use your energy and inspiration to build relationships that promote growth for all in an unconditionally loving way, leaning into resistance with patience and compassion for yourself and others. You are loyal, honest, and transparent with friends and family. Every time you look at your family, you are reminded why you do the work and to keep going! (Mission Statement, Personal Ethos, and Definite Purpose)

It's time to visualize... (Vision Questions)

What is your 25-year vision? What are you doing? Who are you being? How does it feel? (25 Year)

What is your Current Mission? What is Today's Mission? (Current)

How can you take one direct and focused shot for today's mission today? (Today)

At what level are you willing to participate within your family today? (Powerful Question)

One day, one life, Easy Day, you've got this! (Mantra)

You are doing your best, and your best keeps getting better!

Try it on!
Create your morning and evening scripts. Listen for at least 14 consecutive days, and you will notice the messages in your scripts starting to run on their own in your thoughts.

PRACTICE IN ACTION

*"When you bring your full attention to each moment
a day is a complete lifetime of living and learning"
- Mark Divine*

On Jan 1, 2019, I wrote a very detailed vision for my life. In this vision, I wrote about how my relationships would grow with my wife and children as well as friends. I wrote about the strength of my painting company and my involvement in it and how it would provide us with the freedom required so that Heidi and I could build our coaching business and focus on simplifying our lives to make space to do the work—physically, mentally, and emotionally. I wrote about publishing a book and doing speaking engagements all over the country, and so on. I originally wrote it as a 5-year vision. I had the intention of stretching myself; then just for fun, and because I thought it was possible, I turned the 5-year vision into a 3-year vision. I figured, I can create whatever life I desire, so why take five years if three years could be possible.

As I look back at the past few years, I've always had this sense that I was preparing for something. I always felt that the next version of myself was going to be needed to overcome obstacles. Well, here we are in the middle of this most unprecedented time. It is April 2020 as I write this, and the STAY HOME STAY SAFE order is in full effect to combat the Novel Coronavirus. So much is unknown and there is fear in the air, you can feel it. The painting company, our primary source of income, is non-essential, therefore it's parked in the driveway. We also just got the news that Heidi's position as an event coordinator is being reduced and possibly eliminated. And of course the kids' school was cancelled, so we are now homeschoolers.

As we are navigating all of this, there are plenty of opportunities to find the work in each moment. There is constant interplay between the inner domain and external circumstances. We are trying to keep ourselves informed but not get sucked into the fear and political conspiracy theories.   I am aware, moment to moment, of two available voices happening simultaneously. One is feeding fear: *What's going to happen to my business, will I have employees after this, how will the economy recover, should I wear a mask when I get groceries, I just coughed, oh no. The other voice is saying, Breathe, stay calm, and make decisions based on truth, there is an opportunity in everything, we got this, this is why you practice.* Then, the next moment, I have a choice to make.

I had a coaching call with my personal coach just after my business shut down. We talked about the opportunity in being able to slow down, step back, and look at what roles we are playing in the circumstance. To use this time, strengthen your practice and what you stand for in life. Find the hole that needs to be filled in the universe and go all in to fill it. He pointed to the importance of experience; without experience, we cannot turn knowledge into wisdom. We also acknowledged that we are not in control. We can have the highest vision and be doing all the right things to bring that vision into reality and quickly realize there is something much larger at work. The only thing we can control is our inner domain and how we respond. I am reminded of how, many years earlier, I had a vision for my collegiate football career. I was divinely redirected to have the experience I was meant to have. Here we are again in a place in life where the vision is being redirected.

One thing I know for sure is that everything in our life is placed as lessons to learn so we can remember the truth. If we do not grow individually and collectively from each circumstance, we will be presented with another opportunity to learn the same lesson another way. With each passing opportunity, the next obstacle gets more substantial and harder. So today, the work takes on a new meaning—a new level of realization of the importance of doing the inner work as each moment rises and falls. The question arises: *Am I prepared for what is coming next? What version of myself is being asked to wake up? What part of me is not going where we are going?* Here we are in the game of life, being exposed to our weaknesses and character flaws.

Last night Heidi and I were unwinding from the day. The kids were in bed and asleep—or so we thought, until we heard a pitter-patter. Here comes Colton, running down the stairs.

"Dad, I just got the greatest idea! Tomorrow, you and me, let's catch the sunrise."

I checked the forecast, then said, "I'm in."

He ran off, yelling back to me, "I'll pack the snacks."

Heidi and I looked at each other with a smile. I love moments like this, when we realize we are feeding their little souls. The next morning, I gently woke Colton up at 4:45, asking him if he still wanted to hike to catch the sunrise. Our usual spot at home to watch the sunrise is at the top of Saltese Uplands, about a 30-minute hike depending on how often Colton has to stop to check out every rock and any sign of animals. He said, "Part of me wants to sleep, and part of me wants to go." I responded, "It is your choice, What is your heart telling you?" Suddenly he popped up and said, confidently, "Let's do this!"

We were about a third of the way up the hill to our spot. It was 5:15 or so and still dark; Colton was just behind me. He began to sing his favorite song, "The River," by Garth Brooks:

You know a dream is like a river
Ever changin' as it flows
And a dreamer's just a vessel
That must follow where it goes
Trying to learn from what's behind you
And never knowing what's in store
Makes each day a constant battle
Just to stay between the shores
And I will sail my vessel
'Til the river runs dry
Like a bird upon the wind
These waters are my sky
I'll never reach my destination
If I never try
So, I will sail my vessel
'Til the river runs dry...

I joined in and we kept singing, blaring it out.
Absolutely priceless.

A moment later, he said, "Dad, I think I know my purpose in life."

I said, "Oh yeah, buddy, what is it?"

He simply replied, "Love. To spread as much love as possible."

"That's all there is, huh, buddy—love," I said.

He replied, "Yep."

As we arrived at our special spot, Colton asked me, "What now, dadda?"

To which I replied, "Now we practice!"

RESOURCES

Brule, Dan, *Just Breathe,* (Enliven Books, 2017)

Dispenza, Joe, PhD., *Breaking the Habit of Being Yourself,* (Hay House, 2012)

Divine, Mark, *Unbeatable Mind: Forge Resiliency and Mental Toughness to Succeed at an Elite Leve*l (Mark Divine Publications, 2015)

Divine, Mark and Allyson E. Machate, *Way of the S: Think Like An Elite Warrior to Lead and Succeed* (Reader's Digest, 2013)

Divine, Mark and Catherine Divine, *Kokoro Yoga* (St Martin's Press, 2016)

Goddard, Neville, *Feeling is the Secret* (BN Publishing, 2007)

Hawkins, David, *Letting Go: The Pathway to Surrender* (Veritas Publishing, 2012)

Kraftsow, Gary, *Yoga for Wellness* (Penguin Group, 1999)

Lipton, Bruce, Ph.D., *The Biology of Belief* (Carlsbad, CA: Hay House, 2009)

McKeown, Patrick, The Oxygen Advantage (William Morrow, 2015) Ruiz, Miguel, *The Four Agreements: A Practical Guide to Personal Freedom* (Amber-Allen Publishing, 2001)

Simmons, Gary, Th.D, Simmons, Jane, Th.D, Rima Bonario, Th.D. *The Q Effect* (The Q Effect, LLC. 2020)

Simmons, Gary, Th.D. *The I of the Storm: Embracing Conflict and Creating Peace* (Unity Books, 2011)

Singer, Michael, A., *The Untethered Soul: The Journey Beyond Yourself* (New Harbinger Publications, 2007)

Young, Shinzen, *The Science of Enlightenment: How Meditation Works* (Sounds True, 2016)

IHP Coaching www.IHPcoaching.com

Printed in Great Britain
by Amazon

26645662R00069